CULTURE SMART!
KOREA

James Hoare

·K·U·P·E·R·A·R·D·

First published in Great Britain 2005
by Kuperard, an imprint of Bravo Ltd
59 Hutton Grove, London N12 8DS
Tel: +44 (0) 20 8446 2440 Fax: +44 (0) 20 8446 2441
www.culturesmartguides.com
Inquiries: sales@kuperard.co.uk

Culture Smart! is a registered trademark of Bravo Ltd

Distributed in the United States and Canada
by Random House Distribution Services
1745 Broadway, New York, NY 10019
Tel: +1 (212) 572-2844 Fax: +1 (212) 572-4961
Inquiries: csorders@randomhouse.com

Copyright © 2005 Kuperard

Revised 2007; fourth printing 2008

Series Editor Geoffrey Chesler

ISBN 978 1 85733 365 7

British Library Cataloguing in Publication Data
A CIP catalogue entry for this book is available from the
British Library

Printed in Malaysia

This book is available for special discounts for bulk purchases for
sales promotions or premiums. Special editions, including
personalized covers, excerpts of existing books, and corporate
imprints, can be created in large quantities for special needs.

For more information in the U.S.A. write to Special
Markets/Premium Sales, 1745 Broadway, MD 6–2, New York,
NY 10019 or e-mail specialmarkets@randomhouse.com.

In the United Kingdom contact Kuperard publishers at the
above address.

Cover image: Hwangwonjon Pavilion, Seoul.
Travel Ink/Nigel Bowen-Morris

CultureSmart!Consulting and **Culture Smart!** guides have both
contributed to and featured regularly in the weekly travel program
"Fast Track" on BBC World TV.

About the Author

JAMES HOARE spent over thirty years in the British Diplomatic Service, with postings in Seoul and Beijing. His last job was *Chargé D'Affaires* in Pyongyang, North Korea, where he established the first-ever British Embassy. He has written numerous books and articles about East Asia, including *Embassies in the East: The Story of the British and Their Embassies in China, Japan and Korea from 1859 to the Present* (1999), and, with his wife, Susan Pares, *Conflict in Korea: An Encyclopedia* (1999).

Other Books in the Series

- Argentina
- Australia
- Austria
- Belgium
- Botswana
- Brazil
- Britain
- Canada
- Chile
- China
- Costa Rica
- Cuba
- Czech Republic
- Denmark
- Egypt
- Estonia
- Finland
- France
- Germany

- Greece
- Guatemala
- Hong Kong
- Hungary
- India
- Indonesia
- Ireland
- Israel
- Italy
- Japan
- Kenya
- Libya
- Lithuania
- Mexico
- Morocco
- Netherlands
- New Zealand
- Norway
- Panama

- Peru
- Philippines
- Poland
- Portugal
- Romania
- Russia
- Singapore
- South Africa
- Spain
- Sweden
- Switzerland
- Thailand
- Turkey
- Ukraine
- UAE
- USA
- Vietnam

Other titles are in preparation. For more information, contact: info@kuperard.co.uk

The publishers would like to thank **CultureSmart!**Consulting for its help in researching and developing the concept for this series.

contents

contents

Map of Korea

introduction

The past century has not been kind to the people of the Korean peninsula. Nearly one hundred years ago, Japan's defeat of Russia paved the way for the Japanese protectorate in Korea. Then in 1910, the Japanese annexed Korea as a full-scale colony. Liberation in 1945 brought not independence as all Koreans had hoped, but the division of the peninsula that has lasted until today. North Korea attempted to reunify Korea by force in 1950. Outside intervention saved both Korean states from extinction, but the war intensified the division.

Only in the last decade has there been any significant move to heal the wounds of the past. The issue is complicated by the very different conditions of the two Koreas. The North remains a dictatorship, and having once led in economic development and industrialization, is in economic decline. The South, by contrast, once viewed as an economic disaster, built a modern economy in the 1960s and 1970s, weathered the financial storms of the 1990s, and seems well on the road to democracy. The two Koreas are now interacting as never before. Major issues remain, such as the role of outside powers and North Korea's apparent pursuit of a nuclear weapons program. Yet the future looks more positive than it has for years.

The 1988 Seoul Olympics and the 2002 World
Cup, shared with Japan, have helped to increase
knowledge about South Korea, but have not
overcome widespread ignorance about the Korean
people and their culture. Yet those who visit Korea,
whether North or South, will find a place of great
interest with much to offer. Koreans, when not
constrained by politics or other considerations, are
friendly and sociable. The peninsula has areas of
outstanding natural beauty. The South's cities, if not
always beautiful, are vibrant and alive. The North,
while very different, is well worth getting to know.

Culture Smart! Korea shows how Koreans think
and act, and the pitfalls to avoid, and introduces
some of the delights of the peninsula. It is the
product of an involvement that stretches back to the
early 1970s, and of my residence in both North and
South Korea. It derives partly from a little book
called *Simple Guide to Korea: Customs and Etiquette*,
which my wife and I wrote. The European
Department of the North Korean Ministry of
Foreign Affairs, to whom we gave a copy, made this
required reading for all the staff of the department,
since it provided real insights into Korean thinking
and behavior. I hope that *Culture Smart! Korea* will
do the same for many other readers.

Key Facts: South Korea

Official Name	Republic of Korea	*Daehan minguk*
Capital City	Seoul	Pop. 10.4 million
Major Cities	Inch'on, Taejon, Taegu, Pusan, Kwangju, Ulsan	
Area	38,131 sq. miles (98,759 sq. km)	
Climate	Continental, tempered by maritime influences	
Population	47.6 million (2002)	
Ethnic Makeup	Korean: 100%	
Government	Democracy, with executive president and unicameral legislature (National Assembly)	
Borders	Demilitarized Zone between North and South Korea: 151 miles (240 km)	
Currency	Won, divided into 100 chon, but the latter has gone out of usage. The South Korean won has a different exchange value from the North.	Coins are Won 1, 5, 50, 100, and 500. The first two have practically disappeared. Notes are Won 1,000, 5,000, and 10,000.
Language	Korean. People who attended school before August 1945 will have learned Japanese.	
Religion	Traditional: Buddhism, shamanism, and Confucianism. Since the eighteenth century, Christianity has grown, and over a quarter of the population is now Christian. There are a number of new religions, and Islam has about 40,000 followers.	
Media	Thriving press, radio, and TV. Widespread use of computers, the Internet, and cell phones. There are three English-language dailies: *Korea Herald*, *Korea Times*, and the *Joongang Ilbo* supplement to the *International Herald Tribune*.	
Electricity	220v, although some 110v outlets may still be found. US-style plugs are the norm.	
Time	GMT + 8	

Key Facts: North Korea

Official Name	Democratic People's Republic of Korea	*Choson minjujui inmin konghwaguk*
Capital City	Pyongyang	Pop. 2 million
Major Cities	Nampo, Kaesong, Wonsan, Shinuiju, Hamhung	
Area	46,768 sq. miles (121,129 sq. km)	
Climate	Continental, tempered by maritime influences	
Population	22.3 million	
Ethnic Makeup	Korean: 100%	
Government	Authoritarian dictatorship, with unicameral legislature (Supreme People's Assembly)	
Borders	Demilitarized Zone between North and South Korea: 151 miles (240 km). Border with People's Republic of China: 640 miles (1,025 km); and with Russia: 9 miles (15 km)	
Currency	Won, divided into 100 chon. The North Korean won has a different exchange value from the South Korean won. Foreigners have to use the euro as currency.	
Language	Korean. People who attended school before August 1945 will have learned Japanese.	
Religion	North Korea is an atheist state. It is officially acknowledged that there are Buddhists, Roman Catholics, and Protestant Christians, and followers of a Korean religion, Chondogyo.	
Media	All media outlets are state or party controlled. The main newspaper is the party journal *Rodong Shinmun* (*Worker's Daily*). The English-language *Pyongyang Times* is a weekly. There are also editions in a number of other languages.	
Electricity	220v. US-style plugs are the norm.	
Time	GMT + 8	

chapter one

LAND &
PEOPLE

The Korean peninsula has been occupied by two independent states since 1948: the Democratic People's Republic of Korea (DPRK, known as North Korea) in the northern part, and the Republic of Korea (ROK, known as South Korea) in the south. The peninsula curves out from the landmass of Northeast Asia, separating the Yellow Sea between China and the peninsula from what the Koreans call the East Sea. The latter title is disputed by Japan, which calls this stretch of water the Sea of Japan. To the north, there is a long land border with China, and a short one with Russia. The border is ill-defined in places, and Korean and Chinese claims overlap. Between the two Koreas, the 38th parallel originally formed the boundary as set by Soviet and U.S. occupation forces in 1945. Now there is a Demilitarized Zone (DMZ), established by the July 27, 1953, Korean Armistice that marked the end of the Korean War (1950–53). This zone, 2.5 miles wide, stretches some 151 miles on land and another 37 miles through the Han River estuary, right across the peninsula. Despite the area's official title, both sides have brought weapons into their respective sectors from the very start of the armistice, and the DMZ is, ironically, now one of the most fortified regions in the world. For years it was virtually impassable, although recent years have seen some movement across it. One positive side effect of its existence is that much wildlife finds a peaceful sanctuary there, despite the occasional loss to a landmine or weapons tripwire. Some 1,600 plant and animal species have been identified as living in the DMZ, including the rare white crane.

GEOGRAPHY

The peninsula is rugged, with Mount Paektu, in North Korea on the Sino-Korean border, reaching 9,003 feet, while the highest mountain on the South Korean mainland is Mount Chiri in the Sobaek range, at 6,250 feet. Mount Halla on Cheju Island, the highest mountain in South Korea, is 6,365 feet. The whole peninsula is divided by a series of mountain ranges. It is spectacularly beautiful in places, with jagged peaks and fast-flowing streams. This beauty has long been reflected in Korean painting.

The total area of the peninsula is about 85,328 square miles, or roughly the size of mainland Britain. The mountain ranges leave relatively little land for cultivation. Farming and habitation are confined to about 16–20 percent of the total land area. As both Koreas have industrialized since the 1950s, so the amount of land available has steadily shrunk. The heaviest population concentrations have always been on the western side of the peninsula, which also has the best farmland.

There are about 3,500 islands, though some of these are disappearing as both Koreas have compensated for their lack of land by reclaiming it from the sea, a process that originally began in the Japanese colonial period (1910–45). Seoul's new airport, opened in 2000, is built on a mixture of islands and reclaimed land. The east coast has steep cliffs and few islands, and the waters are deep. Far out to sea is Ullung-do, a popular tourist destination, famous for squid fishing. Even further to the east is a small crop of rocks known as Tok-to in Korean, and Takeshima in Japanese, whose ownership is disputed between both Koreas and Japan. (Even more obscurely, they appear on many Western maps as the Liancourt rocks, named after a nineteenth-century French survey vessel.) Tok-to is currently occupied by a detachment of South Korean police. In January 2004, the dispute over ownership of the islands once again became prominent, when Japan objected to a set of South Korean stamps that depicted them, and threatened not to accept letters with the stamps. In March 2004, North Korea announced that it, too, would issue stamps showing the islands as historically part of the Korean peninsula.

On the western side, the sea is shallow, with numerous islands and high tidal variations. Off the southern coast, drowned valleys have produced many islands, creating another area of spectacular natural beauty, with a number of national parks. Further off is the island of Cheju, South Korea's only island province. Its subtropical climate and subtly different traditions have made it a popular vacation spot since the 1950s. Before Koreans had the opportunity to go overseas on such occasions, it was the country's principal honeymoon destination.

Little remains of the original deciduous forests that once covered the peninsula, now replaced by cultivated land or secondary forest. Rice paddy is

the most widespread form of cultivation, even
in the northern part of the peninsula, which is
not well suited to it. Other grains include wheat
and barley, and potatoes are now widely grown
in North Korea. In the South, the use of plastic
sheeting has greatly increased the supply of
winter vegetables. There is some use of it in the
North, partly encouraged by foreign aid workers,
but it is expensive, and it is much less used than
in the South. The southern island of Cheju's
subtropical climate led to the development of a
citrus fruit industry in the 1970s.

CLIMATE

The climate is varied; semitropical in Cheju, where
oranges will grow, but in the rest of the peninsula
varying from subzero winter temperatures to
summer monsoons. Occasionally, winters can be
particularly hard. In the north of the peninsula in
January 2001, for example, temperatures briefly
plunged below -58°F (-50°C), the coldest they had
been for fifty years. Usually, winters are more
moderate, though there are regular spells of
below-zero temperatures between November and
March. Visitors to South Korea will find that
buildings are well heated in winter, so getting the
right balance of clothing is not always easy. In
North Korea, however, while individual hotel

rooms will be warm, few public buildings, even hotels, can supply adequate heating in winter, so it is necessary to bundle up well.

HISTORICAL BACKGROUND
The Three Kingdoms

Koreans trace their historical origins back to the Neolithic age (c. 5000–1000 BCE), when the mythical founder of the Korean state, the half-human, half-divine Tan'gun, is supposed to have flourished. (Tan'gun is regarded as the ancestor of all Koreans, and in the 1990s, in one of the ongoing rounds in the competition for legitimacy between the two Koreas, the North Koreans claimed to have discovered his tomb near the North Korean capital, Pyongyang.) The reality is that it was only much later, well after the beginning of the Christian era, that the first recognizable states emerged on the peninsula. These are known as the Three Kingdoms, of Koguryo, Paekche, and Shilla. All were heavily influenced by developments both political and cultural in China. For a time, the Chinese empire had a number of commanderies, or military colonies, on what is now Korean territory. The greatest of these was Lelang or Lolang (Nangnang in Korean), established around 108 BCE and overthrown by Koguryo in 313 CE.

Claiming the Past

As an example of how the past continually intrudes into the present in East Asia, a dispute has broken out recently between Chinese and South Korean academics about whether Koguryo was, in fact, a Sinic kingdom, and thus to be considered as part of China's history, or, as the Koreans would argue, a proto-Korean kingdom. The dispute arose following a Chinese government intervention to block a North Korean attempt to register certain Koguryo tomb sites with UNESCO as World Heritage Sites. North Korea, heavily dependent on China, chose not to publicize the issue, but South Korean scholars, backed eventually by a somewhat embarrassed government, had no such inhibitions. Separate Chinese and North Korean proposals for the registration of their respective groups of tombs as World Heritage Sites succeeded in June 2004.

Unified Korea

In 668 CE, Shilla succeeded in uniting most of the peninsula, thus helping to create a sense of identity among the peoples on the Korean peninsula that was separate and distinct from that of the Chinese to the north. Shilla's capital was at Kyongju, in the southeast of the peninsula, where there are still splendid archaeological remains to testify to its cultural richness. It was also during this period that Buddhism, also introduced from China, truly flourished in the peninsula. At the same time, the Koreans were absorbing Confucian teachings from China. Shilla was succeeded by Koryo (918–1392), from which, through China, the West learned the name "Korea." Under the Koryo dynasty, whose capital was at Kaesong, now in North Korea, Buddhism become the religion of the court and the aristocracy. Also during this period, Korea made many advances in military science, especially in the use of rockets and other explosives, and also began the development of printing. Raids by Chinese bandits and Japanese pirates in the late fourteenth century increased the importance of the military, which for a time dominated government. But following disputes over how to react to dynastic changes in China that saw the overthrow of the Mongol dynasty by the Ming, one general, Yi Song Gye, staged a *coup d'état*, and proclaimed himself king of a new Chosun dynasty in 1392.

The Chosun, or Yi, dynasty ruled Korea until 1910. The capital was moved from Kaesong to Hanyang (modern Seoul), which became, and has remained, the economic, social, and political center of the country. Under the Yi, Buddhism fell from favor, to be replaced by Confucianism, also imported from China. This new philosophy, with its strong emphasis on social order and education, came to dominate most aspects of Korean life, and its influence can still be traced today. Buddhism never vanished entirely from the scene. In theory, the monks were banished from the cities into remote mountain areas. Even today, most of South Korea's major Buddhist temples are to be found in hills and remote valleys, though the expansion of the cities has brought others back into urban areas. Many kings, even those who persecuted Buddhists, turned to the religion in old age, and it was always strong among the women of the court. Among ordinary people too, Buddhism, with its pantheons of those willing to assist mere mortals, proved more alluring in times of personal distress or general troubles than the more austere doctrines of the Confucians.

Foreign Pressure

Unrest in Korea's neighbors, China and Japan, brought problems for Korea. In the late sixteenth century, under the warlord Hideyoshi Toyotomi (1536–98), the Japanese sought to use the peninsula as a path to conquer China, a move that turned into the long drawn-out *Imjin* wars. The conflicts, from 1592 to 1593 and again from 1597 to 1598, led to Chinese intervention, which saved Korea.

The wars also produced Korea's greatest hero, Admiral Yi Sun-shin, but the fighting left Korea devastated. Large numbers of Koreans were killed or captured. Skilled craftsmen, especially potters, were carted off to Japan, where they helped revitalize the Japanese ceramic industry. Many monasteries and palaces were destroyed at this time, and remained in ruins for several hundred years. Korea suffered again as the Manchu seized control of China and its dependencies in the 1630s and 1640s, and demanded

subservience to their rule. The Koreans acquiesced, but this, too, left its scars.

It was hardly surprising, therefore, that Korea tended to turn in upon itself from the seventeenth century onward, although this should not be exaggerated. Formal contacts were maintained with both China and Japan, with exchanges of diplomatic missions. It was through such missions to China that new intellectual trends flowed in, including Roman Catholicism, which would provoke bitter persecutions in the nineteenth century. In general, the Koreans sought to be left alone. The scholar-officials, versed in Neo-Confucianism, formally despised trade and those who demanded it. The country was thus poorly placed to resist the Western and Japanese pressure that began to build up from the 1860s onward. Two wars, the Sino-Japanese War of 1894–95 and the Russo-Japanese War of 1904–05, were fought over the issue of which country should control Korea. Japan won both. Other powers showed little interest in the peninsula after 1905, when Japan proclaimed a British India-style protectorate over Korea. This was followed by outright annexation in 1910.

Japanese Colonial Rule
There followed thirty-five years of harsh colonial rule until the end of the Second World War brought liberation in 1945. All development in the Korean peninsula from 1910 until 1945 was subordinate to the needs of Japan, a trend that grew worse as the Japanese Empire moved onto an all-out war footing after 1937. The Second World War also led to an intensification of the Japanese campaign to assimilate Koreans into the Japanese Empire. Teaching of the Korean language was forbidden, and Koreans were compelled to take Japanese names.

The Koreans did not endure these developments without opposition. "Righteous armies" opposed the protectorate. On March 1, 1919, Koreans, inspired by President Wilson's rhetoric and hopeful of Western support in the aftermath of the First World War, rose up in a nationwide protest against Japanese rule. The Japanese quelled this uprising with much ferocity. Further protests against the Japanese would occur sporadically, right up to the eve of the Second World War. Koreans in China and elsewhere organized governments-in-exile, marked perhaps more by factionalism than agreement, while in the north of the country and in China, Communist-inspired guerrilla groups fought against the Japanese from the late 1920s onward. A massive Japanese military campaign starting in 1939 drove most of these groups into the Soviet Union or deeper into Chinese territory, from which they would emerge in 1945.

Korea Divided
Korean hopes for the restoration of a unified independent state were not realized. The peninsula was divided into Soviet and American zones, originally solely for the purpose of taking the Japanese surrender. But the wartime allies could not agree on the future of Korea, and the breakdown in their negotiations led eventually to the emergence of two separate states in 1948, the Democratic People's Republic of Korea (North

Korea) and the Republic of Korea (South Korea). Neither wanted the continuation of the division, and there was much jockeying for position along

the 38th parallel, the formal dividing line between the two states. In June 1950, North Korea launched an all-out attack in an attempt at unification by force. It nearly succeeded, but was stopped by United Nations intervention. In the end, after much suffering and great losses, the Korean War only succeeded in perpetuating the division, which still exists today.

THE KOREAN WAR

The Korean War began with a massive North Korean attack along the 38th parallel on the morning of Sunday, June 25, 1950. South Korean forces, many of them on leave, were not prepared for this, and quickly fell back. Seoul, the capital, fell within three days, and the South Korean government retreated first to Taejon, then to Taegu, and finally to Pusan.

The North Korean forces swept all before them. Although, in the absence of the Soviet Union from the Security Council, the United States quickly rallied United Nations support for the

Republic of Korea, this took time to arrive. Some American units were brought in from Japan, but they were lightly armed and proved no match for the North Korean tanks. By August, however, the situation had improved. The North Korean lines were heavily extended, and the line along the Naktong River—the Pusan perimeter—held.

This allowed time for the arrival of more U.N. forces; the first British troops arrived at the end of August 1950, for example, although British warships had already seen action by then. At the same time, the U.N. Supreme Commander, General Douglas MacArthur, the head of the Allied occupation forces in Japan, had decided on an ambitious plan for an amphibious landing at Inch'on, the port of Seoul. This began on September 8, 1950, and at the same time, U.N. forces began to break out of the Pusan perimeter.

MacArthur's forces met little resistance once they had stormed ashore at Inch'on. By then, the North Korean forces were tired and very extended. While there was some fierce fighting as the U.N. forces moved up the peninsula, the North Korean victories of June and August were now reversed. U.N. forces soon reached the Han River near Seoul, and then the 38th parallel. They did not stop but pressed on into North Korea. By late October, the South Korean forces had reached the Yalu River, on the border with China, and

U.N. forces were pressing hard behind them.

The Chinese had been warning since the crossing of the parallel that they would be prepared to intervene. MacArthur discounted such warnings, but the Chinese began infiltrating forces into Korea. On October 26, 1950, the Chinese struck. Before long, U.N. forces were in headlong retreat. Some units fought a rearguard action but many just "bugged out," jettisoning supplies and equipment as they fled from the Chinese "hordes." (One story has it that at a U.N. forces press conference, where the briefing officer had repeatedly talked about the Chinese "hordes," one journalist asked how many made up a normal horde. The term then disappeared from official briefings.)

By January 1951, Seoul had fallen to the Chinese and North Korean forces, and U.N. troops were south of the Han River. Under the guidance of General Matthew Ridgeway, the U.N. forces gradually regrouped and began a counterattack. In April, Chinese attempts to drive them further back failed. Seoul was recaptured and the Chinese and North Korean forces were driven back to the 38th parallel.

In April 1951, President Truman dismissed General MacArthur for insubordination.

MacArthur would later blame the British for his dismissal, but the reality was that he had overreached himself, and the president was no longer prepared to let him get away with overt criticism of Washington's policies. Ridgeway replaced him.

The war now settled into a stalemate, roughly where it had begun. The fighting continued, but now it was more akin to the trench warfare of the First World War than to the earlier war of movement. Truce negotiations began in the summer of 1951. They were soon adjourned, and it would be two long years before an armistice was agreed to in July 1953. At the last minute, the armistice agreement was almost jeopardized by the South Korean president, Rhee Syngman, who refused to sign the armistice and also arranged for the release of large numbers of North Korean prisoners. But despite protests, the armistice agreement came into force on July 27, 1953. It remains in place to this day.

POSTWAR RECOVERY

Recovery from the Korean War took time. Both Korean states were devastated by the conflict. Three million Koreans were killed, wounded or missing, while 10 million families, one third of the population of the peninsula, were broken up.

Thirteen million Koreans, or 43 percent of the population in 1950, were directly affected by the war. The damage was particularly fierce in North Korea, which bore the brunt of the fighting after September 1950, and which was effectively without air cover except in certain remote areas. According to U.S. statistics, the United States Air Force used 386,037 tons of bombs, 32,357 tons of napalm, 313,600 rockets, and 167 million machine-gun rounds against the North.

The North Korean economy was totally destroyed. It had lost 8,700 industrial plants, 906,500 acres of farmland, 600,000 houses, 5,000 schools, 1,000 hospitals, and 260 theaters. In 1953, the North's national income was 69.4 percent of that of 1950, electricity production 17.2 percent of 1949, and coal production 17.7 percent of 1949. There had been a huge loss of able-bodied men, who had either been killed or fled to South Korea.

South Korea was also in a bad way. It had lost 17,000 plants, businesses, and factories, 4,000 schools, and 600,000 homes, and GNP had declined by 14 percent during the war. Total property damage was estimated at U.S. $2 billion, about the same as the country's total GNP in 1949. Effectively, therefore, apart from the end of the fighting, both sides found themselves in the summer of 1953 with nothing to mark and nothing to celebrate. For both North and South

Korea, such victories as there had been had been won by others.

From 1953 onward, the two Koreas concentrated on rebuilding. Both professed their commitment to unification, but in reality neither did anything to bring this about. North Korea recovered more quickly than South Korea, aided by massive support from the Soviet Union and its allies, and from China. By the early 1960s, North Korea was well on the way to becoming the second-most industrialized country in Asia, after Japan. It would maintain this lead into the 1970s, but thereafter began to fall behind. A system based on exhortation and overexploitation of both the workforce and machinery could not continue to produce indefinitely. At the same time, agriculture began to suffer from similar problems; the land could not sustain the constant demand for production. These economic difficulties would remain hidden until the collapse of the Soviet Union and its related economic system, for North Korea continued to receive much aid from this source until 1991.

The North

Politically North Korea also appeared the more successful of the two Koreas, but at a huge cost. Kim Il Sung used the war to consolidate his power, a process that continued into the postwar years. By the early 1960s there was no one to challenge his preeminence, and he would be the ruler of North Korea until his death in 1994. His eldest son, Kim Jong Il, who was probably born in Russia in 1941 or 1942, would then succeed him. But the younger Kim did not assume his father's

role exactly. In a move that struck the outside world as bizarre, the deceased elder Kim became the eternal president. For a time even letters appointing ambassadors were issued in his name, until countries began to object. Even today North Korean officials behave as though Kim Il Sung were still guiding the state. The younger Kim was more

reclusive. His role as Chairman of the Defense Committee would eventually be defined as the highest office of the state, and he became General Secretary of the Korean Workers' Party, though in a somewhat unorthodox way. But he does not occupy the forefront of the stage as his father did. His few trips abroad have been to Russia and China, and have been by train—he is reputed to have a fear of flying, but in any case may prefer not to use the elderly former Soviet aircraft that make up the DPRK's civil aviation fleet. He sees few foreigners and gives no interviews. Kim's own reclusiveness and apparent suspicion of the outside world are reflected in North Korean society generally. Few people have traveled abroad or have access to outside information. With its constant exhortations for vigilance against the enemy and regular air-raid practices, North Korea seems trapped in a hostile past.

Kim Jong Il's succession in 1994 also coincided with major economic difficulties. The disappearance of the Soviet Union and its allies had been a major blow to North Korea. China continued to provide economic support, but periodically indicated that it would not do so forever. Attempts to attract foreign investment proved unsuccessful. Then, in the mid-1990s, a series of natural disasters struck the country. Floods, tidal waves, and drought took a heavy toll on an already weakened economy from 1995 to 1998. The DPRK, in desperation, appealed for international aid. This was forthcoming, but the presence of aid workers, with new ideas and new approaches, led to much tension. Some of the big international organizations, such as Oxfam, pulled out. Many smaller aid groups and the United Nations agencies stayed, but there were constant tensions as the country suffered famine conditions.

These were also the years that saw major international concern over the possibility of

North Korea developing nuclear weapons. The crisis was averted in 1994, partly by the intervention of former United States President Jimmy Carter, but it would rear up again in 2002, and still continues to dominate much thinking about the Korean peninsula.

By 2000, the worst of the famine was over. The world was then astonished by a summit meeting between Kim Jong Il and the then South Korean president, Kim Dae Jung, the first ever such meeting in the two countries' history. For a moment, it looked as though the two Koreas were on the verge of an historic breakthrough. The moment passed, and although the two sides have continued to develop links, the high hopes of 2000 have not yet been fulfilled.

The South
Many dismissed South Korea in the years immediately after the Korean War as an economic failure—the term "basket case" was common. President Syngman Rhee was not interested in economic matters, and was content to rely on international handouts. These propped up the system rather than aided economic development.

A student-led uprising ousted Rhee in 1960, when political corruption finally proved too much for the people to bear. After a brief and chaotic "democratic" interlude, the army seized power in May 1961. South Korea would remain under military dominance until the election of Kim Young Sam as president in 1992.

At first the soldiers had little in the way of plans for the future beyond preventing what they saw as dangerous student overtures to North Korea. Their eventual leader, General Park Chung Hee, had trained at the Japanese Military Academy in the Japanese puppet state of "Manchukuo" in Manchuria and had been an officer in the Imperial Japanese Army in the Second World War. He was also accused of being a Communist in the 1940s but had survived. Park was tough and determined. While he eventually "civilianized" himself and was elected president, there was no doubt that under him military virtues came first.

Park set himself the task of turning South Korea from a basket case into a modern economic power. He had no blueprint and there were several false steps along the way. While presented as capitalism, this was capitalism with a difference. Economic planning, such as the Japanese had used in Manchukuo, was one tool; another was a powerful coercive state, very much on the side of big business.

By the time Park was assassinated by his chief of security in October 1979, South Korea had been transformed from a primarily agricultural country into an industrialized one, well able to match its northern neighbor. Park's death caused a momentary pause in this surge, but it resumed under another military leader, Chun Doo Hwan, and continued until the Asian economic crisis of 1997. Since then, the ROK has resumed its position as one of the leading economic powers in the world, with an increasing concentration of high-tech consumer goods.

The cornerstone of Park's foreign policy was a good relationship with the United States. To this end, Park sent troops to Vietnam in support of American efforts there. He also set out to improve South Korea's virtually nonexistent relations with Japan, and the two countries established diplomatic relations in 1965, after some thirteen years of negotiations. For the first ten years of his rule, Park pursued a hostile policy toward the North, a policy fully reciprocated by that isolated country.

In 1972, however, Park made the first overtures to North Korea since the end of the Korean War, a move prompted by the United States' improved relations with China and the then Soviet Union. Both North and South found that their principal allies were talking to their principal enemies, and in such circumstances seem to have concluded that it was better to talk to each other in case the great powers once again sacrificed the Korean peninsula for their own purposes.

These attempts petered out, and provided Park with an excuse to reinforce the authoritarian nature of his regime. His successors would try again, but it was not until the election of Kim Dae Jung in 1997 that a real breakthrough came. Even if the high hopes raised then did not last, the relationship between the two Koreas has changed beyond all recognition.

Today, there are widespread exchanges between the two Korean states. While the continued presence of large military forces on both sides of the Demilitarized Zone shows that many of the old suspicions remain, and have been reinforced by the North's nuclear program, yet the contacts go on, and slowly understanding, and perhaps some trust, is building up.

Visitors to both Koreas will be made aware of the past. War museums and monuments exist in both Seoul and Pyongyang, and are often on tourist programs. In both North and South, a tour to the truce village of Panmunjom is often a major highlight. Around Seoul, there are many monuments to the U.N. forces, and to the battles of 1950–51. Nevertheless, the growing interchange between North and South Korea is beginning to have a positive effect.

chapter two

VALUES &
ATTITUDES

SOCIAL RELATIONS

The Chinese long ago described Korea as "the Eastern country of courteous people." This aphorism reflected the Koreans' traditional esteem for decorum, courtesy, and propriety, derived from the teachings of Confucius. Neither North nor South would claim to be Confucian in the traditional manner these days, but Korean hospitality, both North and South, is likely to remain memorable.

Koreans do not favor demonstrative behavior in front of those they do not know well. They tend to be remote and may seem standoffish in the presence of strangers. They are not necessarily friendly to people they meet on the street, whether Korean or foreign—though the lost-looking foreigner will often find somebody willing to help.

On the whole, Koreans do not feel obliged to greet in a friendly fashion those to whom they have not been introduced. This is very marked in North Korea, where political considerations also come into play. Korean cities are just as impersonal as cities in the West, and all the traditional rules about courtesy go by the board.

In South Korea, the apparent unfriendliness is perhaps more obvious in Seoul or Pusan, but you will see the same behavior in North Korea among a crowd waiting for a bus, for example. Everybody is a stranger, and so people push and shove in a way that they would not do if they felt that they knew those with whom they were mixing. In this respect, the foreign visitor is likely to be treated just like a Korean.

If you are able to visit a Korean family on their home ground, however, you will meet quite a different reception. There, or in his or her place of work, a Korean will be most courteous and polite to visitors.

GROUP IDENTITY

Koreans can quickly strike up close relationships when they find that they share something in common with a new acquaintance. Among a group of Koreans, especially when meeting for the first time, great efforts will be made to establish links in common. These can be family, school, or university ties, hometowns shared, or even hobbies. The sense of belonging to a group, of being "one of us," is very important to Koreans and plays a major role in developing human relations. It can also exclude outsiders quite pointedly.

As a foreigner, you will not share family or hometown links, but may have hobbies in common, or possibly, in the case of South Koreans, have attended the same university as your host did when studying in your country. This will provide a useful talking point and social bond. In North Korea you may find, among interpreters especially, people who have read a surprising amount of British and American literature. This too can provide a bond, although you may also need to spend some time explaining that London is no longer shrouded in a permanent fog, or that things have moved on since Chicago in the 1920s!

It is very likely that you will be asked a number of personal questions about your age, your education, your religion, your marital status—very few Koreans remain unmarried—and the composition of your family. This is neither "nosiness," nor a wish to satisfy idle curiosity, but an attempt to learn important information that will allow your Korean acquaintances to position themselves in relation to you: to be older, married, and with children, or to have a university doctorate, for example, all give social standing.

In South Korea, you may also find that you are questioned closely about your religious beliefs. Again, this has largely to do with establishing common ground—many South Koreans have embraced Western religions and will be seeking a bond between you and them. Be warned, however, that Koreans, like others in East Asia, differentiate between "Christians," who are from the Protestant tradition, and Catholics, who are not. If you are asked "Are you a Christian?" your interlocutor will almost certainly mean "Are you a Protestant?".

Even today, Koreans frequently use "we" when it is more natural in English to say "I." In both North and South, they prefer to say "our country" instead of "my country" and "our house" instead of "my house." You might even hear "our wife" instead of "my wife"! Don't worry. This too is part of the Korean—and indeed wider East Asian—emphasis on the group rather than the individual.

OLD AND NEW

Some South Koreans at first sight appear very
Westernized. The style of life, especially in the
cities, is similar to that found in other big cities
throughout the world. War and development have
left few ancient buildings. Some modern Korean
architecture draws on traditional styles, but most
is fairly nondescript. In South Korea, you can eat
at McDonalds or Wendy's. Planet Hollywood
came to Seoul in the 1980s, as did the Hard Rock
Cafe. In addition, there are many Western-style
restaurants and shops, run by Koreans, which
show the Korean desire to be modern and
international. Korean men and women wear
Western-style clothes on most occasions.

Traditional costume—*hanbok* in the South,
Chosun yot in the North (both mean Korean
costume)—is increasingly rare, particularly among
men. Just occasionally, a younger South Korean man
will appear in traditional dress, especially at New

Year's. A few wear it at home and it
remains popular among some older
men in the South, who may well don
it for a Saturday or Sunday outing to
the park. There are also some villages
in South Korea where traditional
costume is generally worn.

North and South Korean women
put on traditional dress more

frequently than the men, and it is very becoming.
You will see women in Korean costume at
weddings and the accompanying photographic
sessions, in big hotels and traditional restaurants,
and at cultural performances, but it is steadily
disappearing from everyday life.

RESPECT FOR ELDERS

One aspect of traditional
Korea that has survived is
widespread respect for
those who are older. This
is another inheritance
from Confucianism, which
is still a strong cultural
influence on the Korean
peninsula. To show respect
to the elderly and to those
senior in years is highly regarded. It is therefore
not advisable to sit until those more senior have
taken their seats, and it also makes a good
impression if you stand up when somebody more
senior enters the room. You may find that Korean
young people are reluctant to eat, drink alcohol,
or smoke in front of parents or teachers. If you
are young, or even just young-looking, you may
find that an older Korean abandons you in mid-
conversation to talk to an older colleague. There is

little point in taking offense at such actions. No slight is intended to you.

In theory, at least, this respect for seniority extends to those met traveling on buses, trains, and the subway. In practice, however, the anonymity described above often takes over, and it is becoming less common for somebody to offer a seat to an elderly person. One vestige of the past that you may still find is for those seated to hold the bags of standing passengers. Do not be surprised, therefore, if a heavy bag is quietly taken from you on buses and trains; it is not a thief but a seated passenger wanting to relieve you of your burden for a few stops.

ATTITUDES TOWARD WOMEN

Confucius emphasized respect for the elderly, but he meant elderly men. Neither women nor children ranked very high in his (or his followers') system of priorities. In the past, a woman was taught that in youth, she should be obedient to her parents; when married, to her husband; and in old age, to her son. Much of this has now changed. Some Korean women will smoke and drink (especially if they are over sixty), lead independent lives, and file for divorce. A growing number manage or own businesses. Women are well represented in some professions. Many are engaged in teaching, and there are numerous female pediatricians. In South Korea, women are now admitted to the military academies for officer training, and the South Korean armed forces have appointed their first female general, although, perhaps true to form, she is a nurse by profession. There is a strong feminist movement in South Korea, with departments specializing in women's studies at several universities. A number of women have entered politics, and a few have become ministers.

In North Korea, women have in theory enjoyed full equality since 1948, and certainly, as in South Korea, women are prominent in professions such as teaching and nursing. Women are also represented in official circles and in the military.

Yet the idea of male superiority and female subordination has not entirely disappeared. A middle-class Korean man, whether North or South, will boast that he is a "tiger" at home, even if he does hand all his wages over to his wife at the end of the month, receiving pocket money in return. Women will show subordination to men, especially in public. Korean women, therefore, are not necessarily used to the courtesies shown to women in the West. They will be pleased if a foreigner holds open a door for them or allows them to go first out of an elevator, though they may also be a little embarrassed at the courtesy and unwilling to accept it at first.

A Western woman in South Korea may find that she is not treated as she would be at home, even if she is conducting business in her own right. Usually the courtesy extended to a visitor will ensure that she is well received during ordinary business transactions—she will be invited to lunch or dinner, especially if this is in a Western restaurant. However, she is unlikely to be included in post-work entertainment, particularly if this is to include a late-night drinking session. In North Korea, foreign female visitors will probably not find such discrimination, partly because some of the entertainment outlets available in the South do not exist in the North.

ATTITUDES TO FOREIGNERS

Most Koreans, North and South, are extremely polite to foreigners. If you appear lost on the streets or in the subway, for example, somebody will always try to help. Staff in even the smallest restaurants will do their best to make sure that you eat and drink adequately, even if they have no language with which to communicate. In conversations or meetings, Koreans will be nonconfrontational and will do everything possible to make foreigners feel at ease.

At the same time, Koreans' past experiences of outside interference in the peninsula's affairs have left some suspicions, which may surface from time to time. While polite to individual Japanese people, and often very attracted to Japanese popular culture and Japanese manufactured goods, Koreans remain very suspicious of the Japanese state and its past record, a suspicion that schools do much to reinforce in their teaching of history. Distrust of the Japanese is at its shrillest in North Korea, but it is not difficult to uncover similar attitudes in the South.

There is also a degree of ambivalence toward China. China is, of course, immensely important in cultural terms, and precolonial Korea tended to look toward China for political support and assistance in times of trouble. At the same time, Koreans were very conscious that when helping Korea, the Chinese were not doing so for altruistic motives but because what happened in Korea could have repercussions in China. Recent history has added to the ambiguities in this relationship. For South Korea, after the Communist takeover in China in 1949, and even more after China's intervention in the Korean War, China was a major enemy, allied with North Korea. Since the 1980s, and the establishment of diplomatic relations in 1992, such attitudes have softened, but the memories, and to some extent the suspicions, are still there. In addition, the experience of dealing with China and the Chinese in recent years has not always been smooth; illegal immigration from China has been a problem, for example, and many dislike the Chinese willingness to return North Korean refugees to an uncertain fate in that country.

Not that North Korea is entirely happy with its relationship with China. The North Koreans believe that even when the Chinese have come to their assistance, the Chinese have put their own interests before those of North Korea. So as far as the North Koreans are concerned, the Chinese did not press for a unified Korea at the 1954 Geneva Conference, preferred to reach an accommodation with the United States in the 1970s rather than advance the cause of world revolution, and, perhaps the greatest betrayal of all, established diplomatic relations with South Korea in 1992. And while the North Koreans are aware that they are heavily dependent on China now that the Soviet Union has disappeared, this has added to their resentment rather than eased it. Many North Koreans think that China only supplies second-rate goods and that, if China's needs demanded it, even the supply of such goods would be reduced or cut off.

Suspicion of the West exists, too. It is strongest and most obvious in North Korea, where the focus is very much on United States hostility. Even the food aid that the United States has supplied since the late 1990s has not modified hostile feelings toward the superpower, which have grown more intense since President George W. Bush's reference to North Korea as part of an "axis of evil" in his 2002 State of the Union message. Posters and slogans single out the United States as the principal enemy—though Japan may be shown close behind! The small number of Americans who visit North Korea, however, find that this hostility does not extend to them personally.

In South Korea, too, there is an undercurrent of resentment about the West, again primarily focused on the United States. The United States' presence in the country is very marked. In particular, there have been large numbers of American troops in South Korea since the end of the Korean War.

The American bases are large and occupy prime real estate, and the main base at Yongsan in Seoul is right in the heart of the city. The bases have given rise to entertainment districts, prostitution, and all the other features of garrison towns. In such circumstances, resentment seems bound to build up, and it is regularly fueled by incidents involving American forces. Most of the time, resentment against foreigners remains firmly under the surface, but just occasionally, it comes out into the open. Late evenings can be a time for caution, as young Korean men go home after an evening's drinking. On the streets or the subway, this is a time to be careful. A foreign man with a Korean woman, in particular, may come in for verbal abuse and occasionally some form of physical attack, but any foreigner who stands out, or in some way draws attention, may be at risk. Such incidents are rare, but they do happen. It is best to remain calm and to try to move away from the area.

One thing to avoid is interfering in a quarrel between Koreans, even if it is one between a man and a woman. You will get no thanks and run the risk of getting badly hurt.

Saved by a Korean Granny

One night, coming back to the hotel from a restaurant some distance behind Seoul's Plaza Hotel with my wife, I noticed an altercation between a young Korean man and woman, in which the latter seemed to be getting badly hurt. Perhaps fortified by too much *soju*, I shouted out and went to intervene. In one sense this was a successful move, since the young woman was able to escape. In another it was very foolish, since I— middle-aged, with glasses, and very unfit—was now faced by one very angry, fit young man, who turned his attention to me. I remember briefly reflecting that he had probably been taught unarmed combat during military service, which is mandatory for virtually all Korean men, and would not hesitate to use his skills.

Rescue was at hand, however, because from out of one of the small shops still open, a grandmotherly figure emerged. Perhaps she had been watching, but whatever the reason, she went for the young man and told him in no uncertain terms to go home. Miracle of miracles, he turned away, cursing me as an interfering fool, but departing the scene. The grandmother did not look at us, but returned to her vantage point. I was most grateful, but I also learned an important lesson.

chapter three

BELIEFS, CUSTOMS, *&* TABOOS

Over the centuries, Koreans have shown themselves to be adept at assimilating new religious beliefs. Whether it was Buddhism in the fourth century after Christ, or Catholicism in the eighteenth century, Koreans have been quick to take up new doctrines. In the case of Confucianism, which is perhaps more a set of precepts for conducting public and private life than it is a religion, the Koreans so took to it that they would eventually claim to be more correct practitioners than the Chinese, who had developed it in the first place.

SHAMANISM

A much older religious tradition, shamanism, has survived despite all the new beliefs and all attempts to suppress it. Even today, in the modern city of Seoul, a visitor may come across the *mudang*, or shaman, interceding with the spirit world, and especially with the dead, on behalf of those on earth. Shamanism is not like other religions in that there is no central authority and no doctrine; rather, each shaman is a self-elected specialist. Most are female. Early Korean kings seem to have had shamanistic roles, and archaeological remains from various early kingdoms include artifacts that appear to be linked with shamanism. The famous gold crowns of Shilla are an example, and seem to reflect shamanistic practices in what is now Siberia.

With the arrival of Buddhism (see below), shamanism became marginalized, but it did not disappear. While popular among ordinary people, it also had a following at court during the Koryo period (918–1392). Under the Yi dynasty (1392–1910), which was heavily influenced by Confucianism, shamanism was officially excluded from the court. In practice, however, this exclusion was never complete, especially as far as the women of the court were concerned. Shamanism also influenced courtly music and dance, despite the official disapproval. It survived in the Japanese colonial period (1910–45), but was much discriminated against.

Since 1945, shamanism in South Korea has suffered periods of discrimination. President Park Chung Hee and his military colleagues tried to end shamanistic ceremonies, which they saw as old-fashioned and superstitious. Yet at the same time, "traditional" music was much encouraged, even though it often derived from shamanistic traditions. Since Park's assassination in 1979, shamanism has reemerged into a more public position in South Korea. No figures on the number of shamanistic believers in Korea are available. There is nothing in shamanism that prevents its adherents from following other religions as well, and there are strong links between shamanism and Buddhism.

BUDDHISM

Buddhism has suffered ups and downs over the centuries, but has survived. Introduced from China, according to tradition, from 372 CE onward,

it spread from the Koguryo kingdom in the north of the peninsula to the other kingdoms. In turn, Koreans took the new doctrine to Japan. Buddhism had a profound influence both intellectually and as a source of artistic expression. In the Koryo period, Buddhism was both a popular and a court religion. Many monasteries were built, and members of the royal family became monks. Although few monastic buildings from these early periods have survived, statues and other remains testify to the importance of the religion.

Buddhism suffered under the Yi dynasty, with many of the monasteries being suppressed. Under government pressure, the monks were forced out of the cities and new monasteries were built in remote districts; many survive to this day. But anti-Buddhist pressures were not constant, and even some kings who persecuted Buddhism at one stage would turn to it in old age. By the end of the nineteenth century, Buddhism seemed in decline, with many of its ceremonials and rituals seeming indistinguishable from shamanism. Visiting foreigners described dirty and ignorant monks, and ramshackle monasteries.

Buddhism did survive, reviving in the face of the growing challenge of Protestant Christianity from the 1880s onward. It also survived what many Koreans saw as a too close relationship with the Japanese, though the divisions then created caused problems within the Buddhist community well into the postliberation period. This was partly because some Buddhists were active in the anti-Japanese movement, even if others worked with the authorities. Today, Korean Buddhism flourishes, with about 10 million, or about a quarter of South Korea's population, claiming to be Buddhists. It has adopted some of Christianity's techniques for involving the faithful, and Buddhists have played a prominent role in opposition to dictatorial rule since 1948. Korean Buddhism has also become better known internationally, especially since a number of monasteries have been willing to accept Westerners as monks since the 1970s.

CONFUCIANISM

Whether or not Confucianism should be classified as a religion is a long-standing debate. To some, it was and is more a social and political philosophy, linked to a series of obligations and ceremonies, than a religious doctrine. Others disagree, seeing in the custom of honoring ancestors, and the honor paid to Confucius in particular, elements of religious practice.

Originally from China, where Confucius lived and taught, Confucianism was well established in Korea by the time of the Three Kingdoms. Its approach to the conduct of both public and personal affairs found a welcome acceptance in the Korean peninsula. While the more intellectual concepts may not have spread very far in society, the rules of behavior, and especially the honoring of ancestors, seem to have gained a wide acceptance, admittedly encouraged by the state and local authorities. Until the fourteenth century, Confucianism was not dominant—it competed with both shamanism and

Buddhism for influence—but it came into its own under the Yi dynasty. The new rulers who took power in the 1390s were anxious to restore relations with China. In doing so, they embraced with enthusiasm Zhu Xi's approach to Confucianism, with its emphasis on rites and obligations, which had become the new orthodoxy in China. Other Confucian principles, such as advancement on the basis of intellectual merit alone, received somewhat less attention, or were modified to suit the Yi dynasty rulers.

Today, few formally claim to be Confucian. Yet the precepts of Confucius still predominate in both Koreas. Respect for elders and respect for authority, both derived from Confucian principles, are strongly engrained and encouraged. Whether it is students criticizing the government, or respect for the Leader, elements of traditional Korean Confucianism continue to come into play.

CHRISTIANITY

Christianity came to Korea in the eighteenth century. Korean officials visiting Beijing came into contact with Roman Catholic priests, and took back the doctrines of this new religion to Korea. Not only did they study the books and pamphlets, they also set up a Church of their own. The Roman Catholic hierarchy in China did not approve of this, but it is thus that Korea's involvement with Christianity began.

From the beginning, the state was suspicious of these people who rejected the Confucian rites honoring ancestors, and the persecution of Catholicism began almost as soon as the Church was established. It would continue until the 1880s, and gave the Korean Church a string of martyrs; over one hundred of these were canonized in the late twentieth century. One reason for these persecutions was the link between Catholicism and the Western powers; the Korean government's fear of Catholics was intensified by the clear link between Catholic priests and France.

In the 1880s, Protestant Christianity arrived in Korea. American Presbyterians and Methodists predominated, and have left their mark on the very puritanical cast of many Korean Church communities, in which the use of alcohol and tobacco is very much frowned upon. These missionaries were followed between 1890 and 1910 by smaller groups such as the Anglicans (Episcopalians) and 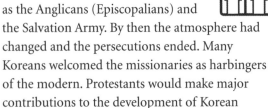 the Salvation Army. By then the atmosphere had changed and the persecutions ended. Many Koreans welcomed the missionaries as harbingers of the modern. Protestants would make major contributions to the development of Korean education and social services such as hospitals, as well as having a profound influence in other areas such as music and the spread of the Korean alphabet, *han'gul*. Christians would play a prominent role in opposition to the Japanese.

Today, South Korea is second only to the Philippines as a center of Christianity in Asia. The total number of Christians, both Catholic and Protestant, is over 12 million, and growing—as already noted, however, the Koreans, like some others, distinguish between Catholics and Christians; the latter term refers to Protestants. Many prominent South Koreans profess Christianity, including several presidents, and Korean churches send missionaries abroad. The Presbyterian Yoido Full Gospel Church claims the largest congregation in the world. His Holiness Pope John Paul II has visited South Korea twice, in 1984 and 1989.

OTHER RELIGIONS

A small Muslim community originally developed among Koreans who had moved into northeast China, where they encountered Chinese Muslims, during the Japanese colonial period. Most of these Koreans returned to the peninsula at the end of the war in 1945, but had no clergy to minister to them. In the 1950s, imams working with the

Turkish forces that came to Korea during the Korean War began to minister to these groups and to make additional converts. The first Korean imam was elected in 1955. The conversion of Korean construction workers in the Middle East since the 1960s has boosted the numbers of Korean Muslims since then. Today, the number of Korean Muslims is around the 40,000 mark, and there are mosques in Seoul and some other cities.

In addition to these mainstream religions, Korea has produced a number of new religions. One, Chondogyo, developed out of the nineteenth-century Tonghak ("Eastern Learning") Rebellion. Today it exists in both North and South Korea, linked to the peasant communities in the countryside. Probably the best known outside Korea is the Unification Church, often called the "Moonies" after its founder, the Reverend Moon Sun Myong (b. 1916). Moon, born in what is now North Korea, was originally a Presbyterian minister, but his Church now is far removed from orthodox Christianity. While it has attracted a considerable following outside Korea, the number of its Korean adherents is relatively small. In South Korea, it has many business interests, and although Moon was for long seen as anti-Communist, in recent years he has visited North Korea a number of times. The Unification Church today has a number of business interests in North

Korea, including an involvement with the Potonggang Hotel and a joint venture automobile factory near Nampo, the port of Pyongyang. The Church has sometimes been favored by the South Korean authorities and sometimes restricted.

The South Korean religious scene today is a vibrant one. The visitor cannot fail to be reminded of this in any Korean town or city, where neon-lit crosses can be seen in abundance at night. Many Koreans remain eclectic in their religious beliefs, however, and just because a person professes one set of beliefs does not mean that he or she will not be interested in and even participate in the activities of other religious groups. This causes no problems with Buddhism and shamanism, or even Confucianism, but Christianity, whether Catholic or Protestant, has tried, not always successfully, to be more exclusive.

RELIGION IN THE NORTH

It is not easy to write about religion in North Korea. Before 1945, the northern half of the peninsula had many Buddhist temples and hermitages, and the same religious mix prevailed as elsewhere on the peninsula. With the arrival of Christianity, the north proved fertile ground for missionary work. Since it was closer to China, new ideas often came into the northern areas first. By 1910, Pyongyang, where several Protestant missionary groups had their headquarters, was regarded as a major Christian city throughout Asia. Pyongyang Foreign School was the school of choice for missionary families in China and Japan as well as those in Korea. Among its graduates is Mrs. Billy Graham, wife of the celebrated American evangelist. Kim Il Sung, North Korea's leader, comes from a family that had Christian connections, and his mother seems to have been a believer.

With the Soviet occupation of the north after 1945, and the establishment of the DPRK in 1948, all that ended. Religion was not proscribed; freedom of religion officially existed, and both the Soviet forces and the new North Korean state tried to make use of some prominent religious leaders to add to their legitimacy. But faith was subject to tight control, and the official line of the Korean Workers' Party, like that of other Communist parties, was that religion was the "opium of the people"—nothing but superstition that had done much harm in the past. Many clergy and believers fled to South Korea, a trend that intensified during the Korean War. During the war, churches and temples were destroyed along with most other substantial buildings.

From the armistice until the 1980s, the North Korean authorities seem to have made no attempt to rebuild religious centers. A few remote Buddhist monasteries survived, but if they were preserved, it was as historical monuments rather than centers of religion. What appeared to be token religious bodies existed, but they were not much in evidence. From South Korea came persistent claims that religious believers in the North were subject to intense persecution.

The late 1980s saw a change. Visitors to Buddhist temples found that people calling themselves monks now once again occupied them. A Roman Catholic church and two Protestant churches were built in Pyongyang, one close to the site both of Kim Il Sung's mother's birthplace and of the church at which she used to worship. A Chondogyo temple also appeared. The religious bodies, long inactive, began to function. The explanation given was that previously, the state had no funds with which to reconstruct the churches and temples destroyed during the Korean War. Now it could afford to do so. It is also sometimes claimed that the lack of such buildings had not hindered those who wished to do so from following their religious practices; they had met in houses or on the sites of former religious buildings.

Since then, many foreigners and South Koreans have visited the churches and temples. Billy Graham preached at the Bongsu Church, while the Vatican maintains a link with the Catholic Church in Pyongyang. In 2003, after North Korea's current leader, Kim Jong Il, had visited Russia, he arranged for a Russian Orthodox Church to be built in Pyongyang, and there are, apparently, worshipers. Whether these are manifestations of real religious belief, or, as some allege, merely actors going through the motions for the benefit of gullible outsiders, nobody knows. Allegations of persecution of true believers are still made regularly among North Korean exiles.

CUSTOMS

Korea's rich religious inheritance has had an effect on its customs and traditions. Whatever their religion, most Koreans observe some form of Confucian ceremony to mark auspicious occasions, even if they do not realize that what they are doing is of Confucian origin. These include the celebration of one hundred days after a baby's birth—a child that had survived so long was likely to live—and the celebration of the sixtieth birthday. Many Korean marriages reflect some aspects of the Christian wedding ceremony, even if it is only in the wearing of a white wedding dress. In South Korea, believers and nonbelievers alike incorporate Christmas and Buddha's birthday into their informal calendar, and even in the North these dates do not go wholly unnoticed.

North and South, shamanistic sounds and costumes linger on in what have come to be called farmers' bands.

Traditionally, the main festivals of the year began with the Lunar (sometimes called "Chinese" in the West) New Year, which falls from late January to late February. This was, and is, a time for dressing up, family visits, and feasting. Although both North and South Korea tried to substitute January 1, and in both that day is still an official holiday and the start of the year, both have accepted that the pull of the Lunar New Year is too strong, and it is now a holiday period throughout the peninsula.

The other great traditional festival was *Chusok*, the fall harvest festival, a time for returning home if possible, honoring one's ancestors, cleaning graves, and celebrating the new crops. In South Korea, it is nowadays an occasion for some of the most spectacular traffic jams and crowded planes and trains, as everybody who is able struggles to get home. In North Korea, where travel is more difficult, few people return home—though if they can, they do. Instead, families picnic in the parks or beside rivers, and in the more relaxed atmosphere of recent years, once again display pictures of deceased family members. They may also bring the ashes of cremated family members along to the picnic.

Formally, public holidays in the two Koreas are as follows:

SOUTH KOREA

January 1	New Year's Day
Late January–late February	Lunar New Year
March 1	Independence Movement Day
April 5	Arbor Day
May 5	Children's Day
8th day of 4th lunar month	Buddha's birthday
June 6	Memorial Day
July 17	Constitution Day
August 15	Liberation Day
15th day of 8th lunar month	*Chusok*
October 3	National Foundation Day
December 25	Christmas Day

NORTH KOREA

January 1	New Year
Late January–late February	Lunar New Year
February 16	Kim Jong Il's birthday
April 15	Kim Il Sung's birthday
May 1	May Day
August 15	Liberation Day
September 9	Founding of the DPRK
15th day of 8th lunar month	*Chusok*
October 10	Founding of the Korean Workers' Party
December 27	Socialist Constitution

TABOOS

All countries have taboos, and the Koreas are no exception. Traditionally, white clothes rather than black were worn for mourning, but this was a special type of white cloth, an off-white hemp rarely seen except at funerals today. A white mourning band is still common, but a black band is also often worn nowadays for mourning purposes. You are in any case unlikely to be invited to a funeral, but you might find yourself expected to pay respects if somebody of your acquaintance happens to die while you are in the country. Usually this will involve attending a memorial hall and solemnly bowing in front of a picture of the deceased.

Many Koreans, like Chinese, still avoid the number four (*sa*) since it has the same pronunciation as the word for death. Thus you will often find that some Korean buildings will not have a fourth floor, or that the letter "F" replaces the number four. Because many Koreans are aware of Western superstitions about the number thirteen, that too may be missing.

Another common taboo is against the use of the left hand to offer an object to somebody. To use the left hand is seen by all Koreans as offensive. It is best to offer something to another person, especially if they are senior in age or rank to you, with both hands. If that is not possible, use the right hand.

Do not stick chopsticks upright in rice, as this resembles the way incense is burned at funerals.

Bare feet are generally to be avoided. Koreans live, eat, and sleep on the floor, so it is important that floors are spotlessly clean. Not wearing socks means that your feet will be dirty. (I have been reprimanded for not wearing socks with sandals by a total stranger on the streets of Seoul!)

If you find that your host is diffident about some issue, do not push too hard. Sometimes a slightly diffident attitude hides a real problem, and if you pursue the issue too much, your host or counterpart will feel a loss of face. Similarly, try not to lose your temper, however much you may feel provoked—you may not feel embarrassed, but your host will.

Gold is the best color for wrapping gifts, and all gifts should be wrapped. Red is is acceptable in the North. Avoid black and white.

Do not touch an adult on the head, or even the shoulder. The same prohibition does not apply to children or youngsters, but on the whole it is best to err on the side of caution and avoid touching any Korean on the head.

Until recently, homosexuality was very rarely acknowledged in South Korea—and it is still not acknowledged in the North. Today its existence is more widely accepted in the South, especially among university students, but you may still find

Koreans who argue that it is something only known in the West. Do not assume that two boys or two girls walking hand in hand are homosexual. Walking thus, or with arms about each other's shoulders, is not a taboo in Korea, merely a sign of friendship. Conversely, a man and a woman who show too much affection in public will attract disapproval.

There are few formal restrictions on photography in South Korea nowadays. Some older people, especially in the countryside, may object to having their photograph taken, and it is best to avoid giving offense. As in many other countries, it is wise not to photograph anything that looks like a military installation or could be for military purposes. This may include airports.

Restrictions on photography in North Korea are likely to be more irksome. The North Koreans have become very sensitive about what they see as visitors abusing their position to take what are seen as hostile photographs—that is, they show the country in a bad light. If you see any sign of hostility, abandon the effort. And of course, avoid any military object, including soldiers, and airports.

chapter four

THE KOREANS AT HOME

There are major differences between home life in South and North Korea. It is not impossible to visit a North Korean house or apartment, but it is rare, and to many people most such visits have a contrived feel about them. Clearly, one is shown only the best and it is impossible to tell how typical are the dwellings shown. If you are entertained in North Korea, it will be in a restaurant, at one of the many guesthouses in Pyongyang, or in a hotel either in the capital or in the provinces. If your business takes you into the countryside, you might be lucky enough to be entertained at lunch or dinner on a collective farm. The best local produce will appear, and there will be much jolly drinking—though some of the liquors produced on such occasions may take a bit of getting used to!

So, most people who meet Koreans at home will meet South Koreans. Unlike the Japanese, Koreans do seem to enjoy entertaining at home; this is partly because Korean houses or apartments are generally larger than those available to the Japanese, especially in the cities.

HOUSING

Most Koreans today live in cities; a quarter of the country's population live in Seoul. In Seoul especially, the favored accommodation consists of high-rise apartment blocks. These blocks, which began to appear in the 1960s, are now all over the city, and they carry none of the negative associations that such buildings have acquired in Western Europe. To Koreans, the tower blocks represent Manhattan or downtown Chicago, rather than the discredited housing estates of London's East End or the suburbs of Paris. The

blocks are safe, with guards, and guaranteed utility supplies and parking spaces. This is the epitome of middle-class living, and most Koreans think of themselves as middle class.

Inside, some attempt at reconstructing aspects of a traditional Korean house takes place. Shoes are not worn, for example, and there may be some rooms in which the family live at floor level; the older members of the family may still prefer to sleep on the floor, while younger people may use Western-style beds. The balcony, if there is one, might have *kimchi* jars on it in winter, as Korean housewives often still prefer to make their own winter *kimchi* (pickled cabbage; see Chapter 5). But there will also be a Western-style sitting room, complete with up-to-date electronic equipment. The furniture will probably be quite heavy in style.

INVITATIONS HOME

If you are being entertained, you will almost certainly start off in the sitting room, with prelunch or predinner drinks and snacks. The latter may well be a mixture of East and West, so expect dried squid as well as Pringles. The meal, however, will almost certainly be Korean food, and may well be eaten in traditional style, seated on the floor. Very few Koreans serve Western food at home even if they eat it outside; most Koreans find Western food rather bland, without the bite of the spices used in traditional Korean food. Drinks served with the meal, however, will probably include beer or wine rather than traditional Korean drinks. As with meals in restaurants, once the meal is over, it is usual to leave fairly promptly. Some Koreans who have lived abroad may offer tea or coffee after a meal, but many will not.

As in the West, if invited to a house, it is polite to bring a gift. Flowers are acceptable, as is

Western liquor. The former can be bought at one of the many flower stalls in Seoul, which will prepare them in suitable fashion; the latter should be from the upper end of the market, and should be gift-wrapped. A book about your country—or your own book, if you have one—is also a good gift idea. Wedgwood and similar products also make acceptable gifts, as do Western-style teas.

Most topics can be discussed on such visits. In the past, politics could be difficult, but the major changes in the political scene since the election of Kim Young-sam as president in 1992 have meant that few subjects are now taboo. If you have been to North Korea, you may well find that your hosts have many questions. The North is still little known in the South, and people are anxious for information. Be warned, however, that many South Koreans remain suspicious of the North, and such attitudes are reinforced at school and during military service. It is probably wise not to appear too enthusiastic on this particular subject!

Even in a social context, many older Koreans will appear somewhat formal. Here, again, Confucian influences come into play; a degree of formality in language and behavior is regarded as the proper course, especially for a senior figure in business, politics, or education. Similarly, formality in dress is the rule, unless you are told otherwise. Do not be fooled by professions of informality; err on the side of a sober style of dress and you cannot go wrong.

EDUCATION

Koreans both North and South attach high importance to education, and they have some of the highest literacy rates in the world. This is partly because the Korean alphabet is so simple to learn and sticks to simple principles. Also important is the very high premium that traditional Korean society placed on education. Education—especially the study of the Confucian classics—was the means of advancement. It opened the doors to government office and thus to worldly success.

Under the Japanese (1910–45), education changed to a more modern curriculum, but few Koreans were able to go beyond the high school level. After independence, both Koreas worked hard to reduce the high illiteracy rates that had prevailed under the Japanese. Today it is almost impossible to find a Korean who cannot read and write. In addition, a massive expansion of educational outlets at all levels began after 1945 and continues today.

University Education

Korea's modern higher education system began in the late nineteenth century with the establishment of missionary schools. A number of these later became colleges and eventually universities. Under the Japanese, a system of state-run universities began, but these were for Japanese people living in Korea rather than for Koreans. Only after 1945 did such institutions become generally available to young Koreans.

Today South Korea has a widespread net of state universities established in every province, with Seoul National University (SNU) at the apex of the system. Private universities also flourish, including many whose reputation ranks with SNU and that also enjoy international acclaim. They include Ewha (a women's college) and

Yonsei University, both missionary colleges. Some are highly specialized, others more general. Altogether there are more than 200 four-year colleges, with nearly 2 million students in South Korea. Many South Korean universities run courses for non-Korean students, with an increasing use of English for teaching purposes. The courses range from short-term training in Korean to full-scale degrees.

North Korea's main center for higher education is Kim Il Sung University, founded in 1946. Young North Koreans eagerly compete for places at this establishment, whose graduates fill many of the top positions in the country. Also popular is Pyongyang University of Foreign Studies. Other colleges exist in Pyongyang and throughout the rest of the country. Foreigners have attended language courses in Pyongyang's universities, and in the past, North Korea trained some foreign students in other disciplines.

International Schools

Seoul Foreign School, founded in 1912 for the children of missionaries, is the oldest international school in Korea. Since the 1980s, it has also had a British School associated with it. There are several other international schools in Seoul, and a few in other cities, including Pusan,

Taegu, and Ulsan. French, German, Chinese, and Japanese schools also exist.

Before 1941, Pyongyang Foreign School, also founded by missionaries, was one of the main international schools in Asia. It has long since disappeared, but in the 1980s, a small Korean-run "International School" for resident foreign children opened in Pyongyang, the only such school in North Korea.

FRIENDSHIP

Koreans rarely refer to somebody as a "friend" unless they know that person quite well. "Friend" in Korean conveys the idea of what is signified by "close friend" in English. Perhaps more than in the West, there is a distinction in Korea between friends and acquaintances. In Korea, "friendship" involves obligations. Most Koreans therefore will have only a handful of friends, often acquired in school and college days or, among men, while doing national service. These friendships and links last. That said, it is wholly possible for a foreigner to make real friends in Korea, and well worth the effort; however, a deep level of commitment is expected, and this may sometimes seem like an encroachment on one's hospitality.

True Friends

Koreans believe that if you are friends, you go along with your friends' wishes, however inconvenient these might be. We found this out one Christmas Day in Seoul, when we had a variety of colleagues from the Embassy over for lunch and then for the evening. Unexpectedly, a Korean colleague telephoned to say that he would be bringing around a group of Koreans to discuss a planned academic seminar to be held early in the New Year. Protests were to no avail, and the group arrived in mid-afternoon. Seemingly nonplussed by our festive hats and clearly merry condition, they stayed for several hours, insisting on discussing the arrangements for the seminar while mince pies and brandy flowed all around. True friends are accepting…

Note that in North Korea, as in China, there is often great play made with the title "old friend." This tends to mean a person who has visited the country more than once, and who has displayed a friendly attitude. "Old friends" are deemed to have indicated a degree of sincerity in their interactions that entitles them to special treatment.

NAMES

The most common Korean surnames are Kim, Lee, and Park, in that order. (You will also find the surname "Lee" romanized as "Rhee," "Ri," "Yi," "Li," and "I," although in the Korean script these are all spelled the same way. "Park," strictly speaking, should be romanized as "Pak," but most Koreans seem to think that "Park" is a better guide to the sound.) Although they may not be related, millions of Koreans share the same surname as a consequence. Families distinguish themselves by their place of origin, such as "Andong." Thus you will find that the "Andong Kims" are a family whose clan shrine is in Andong. Most surnames are one syllable, though there are a few two-syllable ones; "SaKong" is one example. Given names are very important in distinguishing people. Most Koreans have two-syllable given names. Frequently, all the family members of one sex in one generation will share one of the syllables.

In the past, Koreans rarely used their given names. In childhood, their parents would use somewhat jocular and insulting names, designed to prevent evil spirits recognizing and damaging the child. The North Korean leader, Kim Jong Il, was referring to this custom when he referred to himself in deprecatory terms to the then U.S. Secretary of State, Madeleine Albright, in 1999. It is still regarded as impolite to use an adult's given name, and even Korean students will address each other by their surnames, or as brother and sister.

The English terms "Mr.," "Mrs.," and "Miss" are often used by younger Koreans. Older Koreans will prefer official titles, such as chairman, president, professor, or teacher, especially in situations where Westerners might have moved on to a given name basis.

Koreans who have lived abroad, or who have spent a lot of time with foreigners, may be more relaxed about the use of given names. This is especially true of Koreans who have adopted a Western name while abroad, which they can use when they are among foreigners. It is always sensible to check, however, that a Korean acquaintance is willing to be addressed by his or her given name in Korea.

Also note that Korean women retain their own surnames after marriage. Do not be surprised, therefore, if Mr. Kim introduces his wife as Mrs. Park. Some Koreans who have spent a long time in the West may have assimilated the Western practice regarding a wife's name, but it is best not to assume that this is the case.

ACCEPTABLE CONDUCT

Although younger Korean couples may now be seen holding hands in city streets, even in North Korea, older Koreans generally tend not to show affection in public, except to small children. They will not be offended by foreigners exchanging a brief hug or kiss on greeting, but will be surprised if this is repeated frequently. You should also avoid expressions of displeasure. Displays of bad temper are regarded as the height of bad manners and are unlikely to achieve much. It is also best to avoid direct criticism as far as possible. If you have to criticize, do it in a vague and roundabout way, and do not do it in public. The direct approach will leave your audience embarrassed and uncooperative.

Koreans may slurp soup, burp after a meal, and clear their throats noisily, but they do not blow their noses in public. In general, be guided in such matters by how your Korean companions are behaving. You are not obliged to burp if you do not wish to, still less to clear your throat energetically! You will notice that Koreans who have colds will often wear a surgical mask over their mouths and noses.

Many Korean men, North and South, smoke quite heavily, and although restrictions are beginning to arise in South Korea, smoking is rarely prohibited in restaurants and other public places. Foreign brands of cigarettes are available, but are expensive. Younger Korean women rarely smoke, at least in public, but older ones, especially countrywomen, frequently do.

chapter five

FOOD & DRINK

KOREAN CUISINE

The staple food of Korea is short-grain rice, which in the past was sometimes blended with other grains to stretch limited supplies. It is eaten from a ceramic or metal rice bowl with or without a lid. Other tableware includes a soup bowl and various small and large plates for a variety of other foods, often called side dishes. Food is eaten with a metal spoon and a pair of metal chopsticks. Although elsewhere in Asia you will sometimes come across silver chopsticks, the everyday use of metal ones seems to be a uniquely Korean characteristic.

Sometimes you will be given wooden chopsticks in a restaurant. Unlike the Japanese and the Chinese, who use chopsticks for eating rice, the Koreans use a spoon. It is thought to be somewhat gauche to use chopsticks for rice, and under no circumstances stick your chopsticks upright in your rice—this is done only when presenting rice to the memory of somebody who has died. Try to master the use of chopsticks and spoon as a courtesy to your hosts and for your own convenience. In some restaurants, no other implements will be available. The food comes already cut into bite-size pieces, and as a consequence, a knife in particular is considered a coarse object to bring to the table.

Koreans eat three full meals a day, with the number of dishes increasing at each meal. Traditionally, rice, soup, and *kimchi* (see below) appeared at all three meals, which meant that Korean housewives had to be up early to get everything ready before the rest of the family came to the table. Nowadays, many younger Koreans in the cities have turned to Western-style cereals or toast as an alternative breakfast.

In the past, food was served not in staged courses but all at once and eaten together. This was true in restaurants as well as private homes until recently. Before the 1986 Asian Games in Seoul, the government decided that this was wasteful and not suitable for foreigners—who were not consulted—and decreed that all food should be served as separate courses, ordered individually. Gradually, however, the traditional way is creeping back. It is, in fact, easier for a foreigner to order a complete meal than to sort

out the complexities of a Korean
à la carte menu.

You are not expected to
consume everything that is
put in front of you, but try as
many dishes as you wish. Koreans
consider it indelicate to lift the bowl of soup
or rice to the lips as is done in China and Japan,
or to use your hands to pick up food. In a
traditional restaurant and in many homes, food
will be served on low, individual lacquered tables,
with each diner having a complete meal on his or
her table. Diners sit on cushions on the floor.

Kimchi

The most famous of all Korean side dishes is
kimchi. There are many forms of this dish, but the
best known is made up of pickled cabbage
seasoned with red pepper, garlic, and ginger.
Winter *kimchi* was traditionally made in the fall to
last the whole winter and was often the only
source of vitamin C from November to March.
Scientific studies have shown that, while the level
of vitamin C in *kimchi* declines as the winter
progresses, it really does last until March if
properly made in November.

Winter *kimchi* is still made, even in urban
households, although today there are many other
sources of vitamin C available and it is possible to

buy *kimchi* in supermarkets. Its pungent taste and
smell can be quite a shock. In the summer, you
will find mild "water *kimchi*," usually made from
cucumbers in a light brine. There are more than
twenty regional variations of *kimchi*, each
seasoned in different ways. Some caution is
recommended when you first try it, but most
people come to like it. Foreigners find that some
kimchi goes well with Western dishes; roast lamb
seems to benefit from the strong flavor. *Kimchi* is
such an important part of most Koreans' diet that
you should not be surprised if it is served with
Chinese and Japanese food in Korea.

    Kimchi in North Korea is less rich
than in the South, though there are
many local variations. Everybody will
have their own preferences, but we
found that the best *kimchi* we ate in
North Korea was that available around Kaesong, on
the dividing line with the South.

Popular Dishes

These include *bulgogi*, or "Korean barbecue" as it is
sometimes known. Strips of beef are marinated in
sesame oil, soy sauce, garlic, ginger, and other
condiments, and then cooked over a charcoal or
gas brazier at the table. Short ribs, *kalbi*, are also
popular and are cooked in the same way. Koreans
eat much fish and seafood. As in Japan, raw fish,

served with piquant seasonings, is highly regarded.
Many styles of soup are served. Two dishes
formerly exclusive to the royal court now often
appear at special banquets. The first is *kujolpan*,
often called, somewhat poetically, "nine treasure
dish." This consists of small pancakes and eight
special dishes, all presented in a nine-compartment
lacquer dish. You select a pancake and one or more
of the other dishes, wrap the latter in the former,
and away you go. The second is *sinsullo*, an
individual hotpot with beef, vegetables, and a
variety of other ingredients all cooked over live
coals—very hot and very delicious. You will find
that the various ways of preparing food are similar
in North and South Korea, though again, some
traditional regional variations are evident.

Garlic forms an important part of the Korean
diet. It is widely used both on its own
and as part of other dishes. Raw
cloves of garlic will often appear
as a side dish, or for adding to
dishes such as *bulgogi* as they
are cooking. Small dishes of
pickled garlic are also likely to
appear on the table. There is no
obligation to eat this, except on the principle of "if
you can't beat them, join them." After a time, most
people get used to the all-pervasive scent of garlic,
and fail to notice it.

Much hostile publicity in recent years has focused on the eating of dogs and on what are described as other "strange foods" in Korea.

Koreans do eat dog, usually in the form of a soup called *poshintang*, or "body strengthening soup," but it is most unlikely that this would be offered to a foreigner. The dogs, Koreans are careful to point out, are not family pets, but are species bred for the table. In South Korea, dog restaurants and those selling other exotic foods likely to be unfamiliar to foreigners were subject to strict regulation during the lead-up to the 1988 Olympics, but the controls have generally been relaxed since then. Such restaurants are unlikely to advertise their names in English. Few foreigners are likely to be aware of their existence, and they will make no attempt to attract foreign customers.

Less likely to be offensive, but certainly unusual to Western palates, are the numerous wild plants that Koreans eat. These include certain types of bracken, acorns made into a jelly, and bellflower roots. They are often pickled, or served in light brine, and most foreigners who are prepared to try them find that they are quite tasty, and they may even come to like them.

Meals will usually end with plain fruit. In a restaurant, you will often be brought a towel—hot in winter, cold in summer—to wipe your hands on before the meal, and another at the end.

A growing number of Western-style restaurants can be found in Korean cities. In the past, most of these were in the big hotels, but this is no longer necessarily the case. All styles of food can be found, from the ubiquitous hamburger to the most up-to-date French and Italian cooking. Seoul has had a Pakistani restaurant since the early 1980s, and now has a number of Indian restaurants. There are also many Chinese and Japanese restaurants, at prices to suit all pockets. Many are very good indeed. In the provinces, the variety of food will be smaller, except in big cities such as Pusan or Taegu. While it may be possible to eat Japanese or Chinese food, both will be heavily "Koreanized." Western food may be limited to steak, or to the widely available "surf and turf"—giant prawns and steak, a dish that has come to Korea via Japan.

TIPPING
Generally, tipping is not expected. In major hotels and restaurants in both South and North Korea, a service charge plus taxes will be added to the bill. In other circumstances, if you feel you have had exceptionally good service, you can give a small token tip, but this would be unusual.

In recent years, "fusion food," combining different traditions in one meal, has become increasingly widespread, and restaurants serving this style of food are now common in Seoul, though less so elsewhere. It is also increasingly likely to feature in formal banquets in both Koreas.

In North Korea, there are many restaurants available to foreigners in Pyongyang. They include a number of Japanese-style restaurants, an excellent Cantonese restaurant at the Yanggakdo Hotel, and a good Japanese-derived Western-style restaurant at the Potongang Hotel. The latter also has had in the past a good selection of foreign wines, including a magnificent Chablis—though at horrific prices! Most restaurants, naturally, serve Korean food, but a surprising number can also provide a selection of Japanese, Chinese, and Western dishes—the last firmly in the Russian tradition. Outside Pyongyang, the choice is more limited, but visitors are often surprised at just what is on offer.

DRINKING

Koreans like drinking, and there is little social stigma attached to getting drunk, at least as far as men are concerned. Women may find that their Korean counterparts, especially older women, do not drink much alcohol, although there are exceptions. Drinking parties, especially among men, are common and very popular. Younger people, especially students, will now drink in mixed groups. A few drinks shared in a bar with Korean acquaintances will go a long way toward establishing friendships. Koreans do not as a rule drink alone, and they do not drink much without eating fairly substantial snacks called *anju*. This does not stop them getting drunk, however, and drinking parties may often become quite boisterous. Such sessions may be used to let off steam and to criticize the boss to his face, but without the dire consequences this might have in the West. The convention is that remarks made at drinking parties are not referred to the next day.

When drinking, even in an informal setting, you should not pour your own drinks. You should hold your glass in front of you, with both hands or with the right hand supported under the elbow by the left hand, and allow the host or somebody else to pour for you. Similarly, you should offer to fill other people's glasses in the same way. If somebody toasts you, they will probably drain their glass. You should do the same, at least on the first occasion.

You might be offered beer with your meal, or a soft drink. *Poricha*, or barley tea, a way of ensuring that water has been boiled, is particularly popular in South Korea. It is served hot in winter and cold in summer. It seems to be unknown in North Korea, where beer and soft drinks will usually be available.

At more formal functions, Western-style wine may be available in both North and South, as well as some form of spirit-based drink. The quality of wine will vary a lot. In South Korea, there is a small domestic wine industry, producing mainly German-style white wines, but good quality foreign wines are also available at a price. In North Korea, the choice is more limited, and some very bad wine has been around in the past. In recent years, more drinkable wines, including wines from Latin America and Australia, have appeared in shops catering to foreigners. These may sometimes appear at formal occasions.

Beer is very popular in South Korea. There are several well-known Korean brands, including OB, Hite, and Cass, and a number of variations, though most Korean beer is German-style lager. Foreign brands, usually brewed in Korea under license, are also widely available in the big cities, at a price. Heineken, Budweiser, and Carlsberg are popular foreign brands. Some hotels offer even more exotic foreign beers, including both Guinness and British-style draft beer. As mentioned above, Western-style wine is made in South Korea. The white tends to be better than the red. French, Italian, American, and

Australian wines can be found in restaurants, and are often now on sale in hotel shops, in both the big department stores and smaller supermarkets and convenience stores, and, in Seoul and some other cities, in specialist wine shops. Whiskey and gin, both imported and locally produced, are widely available. Foreign brands are expensive, especially in hotels, where they are best avoided. Johnny Walker Black Label and Chivas Regal are particularly well-known brand names among Koreans, and they make good presents.

Traditional Korean alcoholic drinks are everywhere giving way to their Western competitors. They are worth sampling, however, if you get the chance. The most common ones are *soju*, the cheapest, generally the strongest, and rather like vodka, though often only about 25 percent alcohol by volume; *makkoli*, a milky-white drink, sometimes compared to beer, and now getting rarer; and *chong-jong*, a rice wine, similar to Japanese saké and, like saké, usually served hot, although it is common nowadays to find it served cold in summer. *Popchu*, a higher-quality saké-like drink, is well worth seeking out.

Much of the above also applies to North Korea. Scotch whiskey is popular, especially but not exclusively among those who have traveled or lived abroad. Even remote hotels are likely to come up with a bottle or two of Scotch. Beer is widely available, much of it made locally. In Pyongyang, there are a number of microbreweries in hotels and restaurants. The recent acquisition of a former Usher's brewery from England, together with German techniques, has led to a much improved quality of bottled beer in the capital at least. Foreign beers, especially from Japan or China, are often available.

In the past, Korean women did not drink until they were over sixty. Today, it is not unusual for a Korean woman to take a glass of wine at dinner, though most still stick to orange juice. A few will drink quite a lot. However, women rarely get drunk—it is bad form for them to do so—and a Western woman will need to take this into account. In any case, as mentioned, a Western woman is unlikely to be invited to the more riotous parties. Although Korean men and women traditionally socialize mainly with their own sex, they generally understand Westerners' expectations of a mixed social gathering.

If you do not drink, do not worry. There are many Koreans who do not drink alcohol. Many "Christians" do not touch alcohol. It is also well understood that those taking certain medicines should avoid alcohol. More recently, random breath tests by the police have persuaded many South Koreans not to drink and drive. So if you wish to be excused, you can plead that you have religious convictions, that you are taking medication, or that you are driving.

TOASTS

At formal meals, the custom of toasting is very popular. Formal toasts and formal speeches, if there are to be any, may well take place at the beginning of the meal, before any eating has begun. On such occasions, the principal host and the principal guest will normally propose and respond to the toasts. You should note that while it is usual to drink beer, wine, and soft drinks as you wish, the spirit glass is normally reserved for drinking toasts. Often this will be Scotch whiskey, though traditional Korean spirits such as *soju* may sometimes be served. Faced with a number of alcoholic drinks, the best thing is to follow the principals, using the wineglass if they do, for example. Thereafter, it is not uncommon for there to be regular toasting during the meal. Sometimes this will involve everybody, but sometimes it will just be individuals who toast each other. In all-male company, this can become quite a competition, and men may feel much pressure to drink large amounts of strong liquor. It is customary to turn the empty glass upside down, to show that the contents have been consumed. In mixed company, there is likely to be less pressure to drink; women need not feel compelled to drink toasts—they can simply touch the glass to their lips.

As in other parts of East Asia, it has also been customary to exchange glasses when drinking. This was seen as a mark of friendship. In recent years, the practice has become less common because of the realization that such exchanges could spread diseases.

RETURN HOSPITALITY

When you leave a restaurant or bar, you will not normally need to worry about the bill if a Korean colleague has invited you. You are the guest, and taking care of the bill is your Korean host's responsibility. Koreans generally do not like the Western custom of "eating together and paying separately." The best way to repay hospitality is to invite your Korean friends to dinner after you have been entertained a couple of times. Take advice on both venue and costs—the latter can be very high.

If your Korean counterpart is visiting your country, that may well be a better opportunity to repay hospitality, perhaps even in your own home.

TIME OUT

ENTERTAINMENT

Visitors or residents in South Korea will not lack for things to do. Activities range from eating and drinking in a bewildering range of establishments, through the opportunity to sample the highest international culture and a variety of museums and galleries, to floorshows of all types. Availability varies, of course. Seoul is very much at the apex in all that is on offer, and all interests are catered to in that city, but all the big cities will offer something.

Information about what is on is readily available. Seoul had two English-language newspapers for many years, the *Korea Herald* and the *Korea Times*. The former was long associated with the government, and the latter with the opposition, but it was hard to tell them apart. In recent years, not only have both gone online, but they have also been joined by a number of other English-language papers, some linked to Korean dailies. They provide details of concerts and other forms of entertainment, which are also advertised on posters and billboards around the city.

In Seoul, the number of theaters and concert halls has increased steadily since the 1970s, stimulated by economic success and international events such as the 1988 Olympic Games. Even in the 1980s, it was said that there was a performance of Shakespeare in one or other of Seoul's many theaters every night of the year. By now, there must be two or three. Much experimental theater can also be found. Korea did not develop in theatrical terms as did Japan and China, and nothing quite matches *kabuki* or Peking opera in the Korean tradition. But traditional performances of mask dances and other folk traditions are widely available and increasingly popular, as are performances of the various styles of Korean

traditional music, from stately court performances to the exuberant drumming of the farmers' bands. These are often packaged for foreigners, with a traditional Korean dinner accompanying the music and dance.

Koreans have taken to Western music in a big way, and performances abound. Classical Western music is also available on the radio, and sales of compact discs are very high; whether the artists are Korean or foreign, compact discs are a good bargain, and an enjoyable souvenir. As well as numerous high-quality indigenous orchestras

and performers, there is a
steady stream of famous
international visitors to add
to the variety. Foreign classical
orchestras find an enthusiastic
audience in Korea, but the
international pop scene is also well
represented, and jazz, partly spurred on
by the large American presence in the country, has
many outlets, especially in areas frequented by
off-duty American servicemen. Be aware,
however, that such areas are not always the most
salubrious, especially as the night moves on.

Art galleries abound, covering traditional
Korean styles of art and much more besides. A
vibrant tradition of experimental art, once
frowned upon by the authorities, now attracts
wide audiences. Foreign art is widely available
today, in contrast even with the early 1990s.

The cinema is very popular, and Seoul has many
movie houses. A strong Korean film industry, which
can trace its origins back to the 1920s, has begun to
win international prizes, but many foreign films are
also shown to enthusiastic local audiences. Once
foreign films were dubbed into Korean, but today
this is no longer the case, except on television.
Today, foreign films shown to a Korean audience
will have subtitles. Since the end of military
dominance in politics following the election of Kim

Young Sam as president in 1992, foreign films dealing with political themes are no longer banned.

Seoul has an abundance of museums. There are museums devoted to *kimchi*, the essential Korean condiment, to stones, to wrapping clothes, and to a host of other specialized interests. Most universities have museums, which, in the case of private establishments such as Korea or Yonsei universities, may reflect the particular interests of the founders. There is a fascinating National Folk Museum in the grounds of Seoul's Kyongbok Palace, which traces the life and customs of people of all classes and occupations up to the end of Korea's independence in 1910. Not to be missed is the Korean War Memorial, part shrine, part museum, which has been built on a former part of the United States military base at Yongsan. It takes as its theme all of Korea's past conflicts, not just the 1950–53 Korean War.

Outside Seoul, there are many museums to be found throughout the country, in addition to the local branches of the National Museum. Again, many are based in universities, but they can also be found in monasteries and at historic sites.

THE NATIONAL MUSEUM

The National Museum of Korea is a countrywide establishment, with the main museum in Seoul and branch museums in all the major cities. The best of these is probably that at Kyongju in the southeast, but all are worth a visit. Once they were quite old-fashioned in their presentations, but increasingly they are being rebuilt or updated, with modern styles of display and layout.

The Seoul museum has suffered because of political decisions. Originally established in 1908 in the final years of the Yi dynasty, it was developed by the Japanese. In 1945, the museum became the National Museum of Korea, with buildings in the Kyongbok Palace in Seoul. During the Korean War, the North Koreans intended to take all its holdings to the North in 1950, but Seoul's recapture took place before they could do so, and the museum, like the government, sat out the war in Pusan. At the end of the war, it moved back to Seoul, and in 1972 moved into a new building in the Kyongbok Palace grounds. However, in 1986, the Museum moved to the former Japanese administrative offices, known as the Capitol Building, in front of the Kyongbok Palace. This made a surprisingly good museum. For the first time, most of the collection was on display. In 1994, however, President Kim Young Sam decided that the Capitol Building was too painful a symbol of the colonial past, and decreed that it should be destroyed. The museum, whose staff were not consulted, was forced to move into temporary buildings that it has occupied ever since, its former building in the palace grounds having become the Folk Museum. A new building is promised, but has not so far materialized.

The collection is very rich, especially in archaeological materials from the various excavations of royal tombs throughout the peninsula. It is strong in statues of the Buddha, and in Korean painting.

For those staying longer in Seoul, the Korea Branch of the Royal Asiatic Society (KBRAS), originally founded in 1900, runs a regular series of lectures on the culture and history of the peninsula. The society's membership over the years has included most of the well-known names in Korean scholarship, including many prominent Korean scholars. It publishes an annual volume of *Transactions*, which is the oldest journal in the world devoted to Korean studies. In addition to its lecture series, which is aimed at the nonexpert, KBRAS has regular excursions to scenic and historic sites throughout South Korea (and nowadays to China and other neighboring countries as well). These outings, with knowledgeable guides, are a good way to see the more unusual aspects of the country and also to get to know both Koreans and the resident foreign community.

SPORTS

Both traditional and modern sports are available. The former includes Korean-style wrestling, *ssireum*, and taekwondo, the Korean version of unarmed combat. The latter is also a popular participation sport among foreigners. Spectator sports include baseball, and more recently, soccer, especially since the 2002 Football World Cup, jointly hosted by the Republic of Korea and Japan. The World Cup created much local enthusiasm (also echoed in North Korea), and soccer is now firmly established as a Korean sport. The armed forces play rugby, but this sport does not otherwise have much of a domestic following except among expatriates. Horse racing enjoys some popularity, as does horse riding.

Skiing, which became popular in the late 1970s and early 1980s, has now taken off in a big way, with several world-class ski resorts, most within easy reach of Seoul. Once accommodation and other facilities were relatively simple, but nowadays they reach the highest international standards. The season lasts from December to early March, although the resorts open from the end of November.

Golf is probably the most popular sport in South Korea, even if many of those who claim to be golfers rarely get beyond the driving ranges that can be found in the cities. Golf can be very expensive; it has always been especially popular among the industrial leaders of the country, perhaps in imitation of their Japanese counterparts. As in Japan, it can be particularly expensive for the outsider, and most foreign residents probably only play when invited by a Korean host. That said, if you have golf clubs and expect to do business, bring them to Korea. Many hotels have links to golf courses, and their guests can play on them. A lot of business can be done on the golf course, and Koreans are usually very pleased to find that a foreigner shares their passion for the game.

FURTHER AFIELD

There is a huge range of scenic spots to visit, from Cheju Island in the south to the mountains of the east coast. All over South Korea, the discerning traveler will find places of amazing scenic beauty, with landscapes (and seascapes) that change dramatically with each season. Hiking trails snake up into the hills, or along coastal paths. Temples or hermitages, often dating back a thousand years or more, even if the structures you see are relatively new, are to be found everywhere. Not only are the buildings attractive, with their curving roofs and stone pagodas, but since they provide popular destinations for Koreans, they will also give you a good opportunity to see Koreans enjoying themselves. And they do, singing, dancing, and drinking, men and women—and foreigners, if they can be dragged into the fun!

Areas once restricted, especially on the east coast, because of fear of North Korean infiltrators, are now readily available to Koreans and visitors alike. The east coast has splendid beaches, with miles of golden sands. The west coast is equally attractive, with small islands—some tidal— situated close inshore. A steady increase in the number of National Parks has been accompanied by major improvements in access, facilities, and accommodation.

SHOPPING

Shopping can be great fun in South Korea, whether in the big cities, with their smart department stores and numerous markets, or in small local markets. The range of goods available is huge, with CDs and electronic goods proving especially popular. Leather and brass products are also of a high standard. The country markets may well specialize in excellent traditional products, such as the bamboo goods at the village of Tamyang in South Cholla province. While prices may be fixed in the big department stores, they are not in the markets or in other shops, such as those in Itaewon near Seoul's American base, and bargaining is quite normal. Itaewon has the advantage for foreigners in that the shops and services such as tailors have grown accustomed to providing for the U.S. military and their families, and will stock or supply goods in larger sizes. Even though South Koreans are becoming bigger as they move from the traditional diet to a more Westernized one, they are still generally smaller than their Western counterparts.

Itaewon is also a center for traditional Korean-style furniture. Real antiques can be found in the area known as "Mary's Alley," near the Kyongbok Palace in the city center, but they are expensive. You are unlikely to find a real antique in Itaewon except at comparable prices to Mary's Alley, but a wide range of copies, some good, some less so, will be available.

You will find bookshops selling foreign-language books, including books about Korea, at a number of places in Seoul. The Kyobo Book Center is a vast underground shop right in the heart of the city. As well as books, it has CDs, computer software, and a wide range of stationery. Another good bookshop is at the Ulchiro 1-ga subway station. The Royal Asiatic Society Korea Branch publishes and sells books; they are available at a discount to members.

Duty-free shops, with international brands and high-quality Korean goods, are available in a number of big cities, as well as at the international airports. Prices are comparable to those elsewhere.

Some visitors may like to try two traditional Korean experiences, the barbershop and the bath. Korean barbershops can be a very pleasant experience. You may not be able to appreciate the political and other gossip, but the combination of haircut, shave, and massage that usually features in a Korean barbershop's repertoire is quite an experience. It is a good idea, however, to stick to barbershops in hotels or other central locations. Sometimes other establishments can be a front for prostitution. As such, they have been the target of frequent government campaigns against "lewd practices."

Korean public baths are similar to those found in Japan, with large communal bathtubs. Where they

survive, they will now often offer specialized pools.
As South Korea becomes wealthier, they are
being supplanted by similar, but more
expensive, "saunas," often in the bigger
hotels. Public baths are segregated. They
are friendly places, where inhibitions
disappear. As in Japan, you must soap and
rinse yourself thoroughly several times
before entering the main bath. Again as in Japan,
this is likely to be at a hotter temperature than most
Westerners are accustomed to, and you should be
careful. Sit still and the pain eases! Many baths are
equipped with saunas and resting rooms. In certain
parts of the country, a variant of the bath is the hot
spring, where natural water provides a means of
relaxation and rejuvenation. Hot springs can be
found all over the country, and today they are often
fitness centers with elaborate gym facilities.

THE NORTH

North Korea is rather more limited in what it has
to offer, and visitors will have far less choice in
what they do or see. Much will depend on what
you have asked to see before you go, though some
sites tend to be a standard feature of all tours. All
visitors will be accompanied by one or more
guides. Their role is to make your visit as smooth as
possible, but they will also try to ensure that you do

not see or do anything that the authorities would rather you did not. Some "minders" can be helpful and understanding. Most will err on the side of caution with you. Remember, even if your guide is not around, other people will be watching you.

Of course there are museums and art galleries, especially in Pyongyang. It is not easy just to visit these. Indeed, the only museum that seems to accept the casual visitor without advance warning is the Folk Museum, situated not far from Kim Il Sung Square. This is smaller than its Seoul counterpart, but equally good in its depiction of life from prehistoric times to the end of the Yi dynasty in 1910. Other museums include the History Museum, the Revolutionary War Museum, and the Fatherland Liberation War Museum, devoted to the Korean War. All are worth a visit, although the style and content will strike most Westerners as very old-fashioned. There are also art galleries, and you can visit the display center of the Three Revolutions (in arts, science, and philosophy) by arrangement.

Pyongyang has many set-piece monuments, to which visitors are taken. Most prominent is the large gilded statue of Kim Il Sung that stands on Mansu Hill. Here Koreans and foreigners come to lay flowers before the Great Leader. One can decline to do so, but your North Korean hosts may be disappointed at such an action. They will, in any case, expect you to behave with decorum. Other sites associated with Kim Il Sung to which visitors are likely to be taken include the Arch of Triumph, marking the spot where he is supposed to have addressed the citizens of Pyongyang on liberation in 1945, his birthplace just outside the city at Mangyongdae, and the Kumsusan Memorial Palace, where his embalmed body lies in state. Kumsusan is open twice a week, and foreigners are welcome. A visit involves elaborate checks and controls, to make sure that no contamination enters the building. Visitors should also be neatly dressed, with no bare arms. Be warned that overcoats, scarves, and hats must all be given up on entry. Kim's birthplace at Mangyongdae is more relaxed. It is set in an attractive park, with pleasant walks. At these and other monuments and historic sites, a guide will provide the official account of what is deemed significant.

Despite journalists' descriptions of it as a "Stalinist city," Pyongyang has much to recommend it. There are many parks and green spaces, and delightful riverside walks along the Taedong and the Potong Rivers. On weekends, people will be picnicking, with dancing and singing, just as they would be in the South. Overzealous minders sometimes prevent visitors from just wandering about, though this has eased somewhat in recent

years. Shopping is not the delight that it is in South
Korea. Foreigners may visit shops out of curiosity,
but most find that there is little they would want to
buy, even if they could. Revolutionary posters,
available at the Foreign Languages Bookshop, do

make attractive gifts. However, those
same overzealous guides have been
known to deny the existence of the
bookshop, and persistence may be
required to visit it. There is a duty-
free shop at Pyongyang airport, with
a small selection of liquors. The
airport also has a more general
souvenir shop and a bookshop.

The theater, a musical performance, or one of
the two circuses make good outings, but may not
always be available, especially in winter, when
theaters and other places of entertainment are not
heated. It is always worth asking, however. The
"revolutionary operas," which perhaps owe more
to the Chinese tradition than to any Korean one,
are well staged and very dramatic. If foreigners are
attending, the texts may be projected in English at
the side of the stage.

Occasionally, you will come across a poster for a
concert or some similar event, but finding out what
is on, and what may be available for foreigners, is
no easy task. "Keep asking" seems to be the rule.

What are called "mass games" or "mass

gymnastic performances" are worth seeing. Thousands of people working together provide spectacular set pieces based on the exploits of Kim Il Sung or other aspects of recent history. Otherwise, nightlife is generally confined to restaurants and hotel bars; the latter sell a variety of local and imported beers and spirits. There are restaurants and bars available on one or two boats moored along the Taedong River, and these provide an attractive setting on a summer's evening.

Away from Pyongyang, visitors will find that North Korean scenery is every bit as stunning as that in the South, though there is nothing like the South's tourist infrastructure. Unfortunately, the Kumgang or Diamond Mountains, on the east coast, one of Korea's most famous beauty spots, are not at present accessible to foreigners in North Korea. Not much in the way of historic buildings survived the Korean War, but there are some reconstructed temples and hermitages. Mount Myohyang, about 75 miles (120 km) north of Pyongyang by road, has some Buddhist remains, excellent hill walking, and two museums devoted to preserving the gifts given to both Kim Il Sung and Kim Jong Il. All are worth visiting. Kaesong, on the division between North and South, not only provides access to the truce village of Panmunjom, but is also one of the few North Korean towns to have preserved many of its older buildings.

TRAVELING

GETTING AROUND IN THE SOUTH

Visiting South Korea is relatively straightforward.
Most Western countries have visa waiver
arrangements with the Republic of Korea, usually
allowing visits of up to 90 days. Those going for
work will need visas, but these are easily obtained
from ROK Embassies around the world.

South Korea has a modern and highly
developed transport system. Most visitors will
arrive in the country at the Inch'on International
Airport, a stunningly designed facility opened in
2000 that has been built on reclaimed land and an
island offshore. Its only drawback is that it is not
yet on the subway system, but this will change in
the next few years. Taxis and buses provide
frequent links to Inch'on city, where the subway
system runs, or to the center of Seoul. There are
also international flights from Pusan and some
other airports. Seoul's domestic airport, Kimpo,
has subway connections to the city center. South
Korea's two carriers are Korean Air, the oldest,
and Asiana Airlines, but most major airlines also

serve the country, with a small number flying to Pusan as well. Departing passengers will pay a tax, now included in the price of the ticket.

Boats

A few people come by ship to Inch'on, which has sea links to China and North Korea—there are direct services for freight to the latter, but passengers have to take a ferry to Dandong on the Chinese side of the Yalu River, and then cross to the North Korean city of Shinuiju to catch the train. From Pusan, there are ferries to Japan. Ferries also connect the Korean mainland with Ullung Island in the East Sea and with Cheju and other islands off the south coast. They can be a fun way to travel and get to know people. The local ones in particular may not have much in the way of comfort, however, and the seas both east and south can often be rough.

Trains

Railways began to appear at the start of the twentieth century and were much expanded during the Japanese period. They suffered badly during the Korean War, and the modern railway system is smaller than its prewar predecessor. That said, most main cities are accessible by rail. Seoul and Pusan are linked, since April 2004, by a fast French-designed bullet train, which has reduced the journey time to two hours and forty minutes from the previous four hours. Not only are these trains modern and fast, they are also cheap by European or North American standards—the single fare to Pusan is about £20 or $30. Visitors can purchase Korean Rail passes outside the country, allowing unlimited travel for set periods, which further reduces the cost.

Road Transportation

The road system also dates from the Japanese period. Korean roads were traditionally very bad. In the 1950s and 1960s, it was easier to fly to many places than to drive, and many small airports sprang up all over the country. Even twenty-five years ago, a surprisingly high proportion of roads were still dirt tracks, but this has changed in recent years. A major construction program from the early 1970s saw the spread of modern high-speed roads. This also led to a countrywide system of fast buses, which provided a much cheaper service than by air, and many airports were closed.

But from the mid-1980s onward, the pendulum swung again in favor of flying. Car purchase, hitherto very expensive, was encouraged to boost the faltering automobile manufacturers, and car ownership became widespread. As a result, the sheer volume of traffic on the roads has often reduced progress to a miserable crawl. This was especially the case at major festivals, such as the fall harvest festival, *Chusok*, or Lunar New Year, when many people return to their ancestral homes. Friday and Sunday evenings are still likely to produce major jams, especially around Seoul, so the wise traveler will choose an alternative to road travel wherever possible.

Within cities too, the volume of traffic means that journeys by road can be very slow and time-consuming. It is possible to rent cars, with an international driver's license, but visitors contemplating doing so should remember that the Korean style of driving is somewhat different from that practiced elsewhere, and parking may be a difficulty. Many middle-class Koreans still have chauffeurs, so parking is less of a worry for them, but somebody unfamiliar with Seoul or Pusan may well find themselves experiencing problems. Traffic police were once indulgent toward foreigners who parked illegally or badly, but those days have gone. If you do decide to drive, finding your way about is not such a problem, as most signs include names in roman script. Be warned that U-turns are only allowed at certain designated points, and you may sometimes have to go well out of your way to turn around.

All major South Korean cities have good bus services, though they, too, suffer from the density of traffic. Many foreigners use the buses, though it is useful to have some knowledge of Korean to do so, since destination boards are not usually in roman letters. Be warned that bus stops are often a long way apart—miss your stop and you will have a long walk back!

The Subway

By far the best way to travel is the subway system, especially in Seoul, where the subways provide comprehensive coverage of the city. Other cities also have subway systems, but none is as highly developed as that of Seoul. The lines stretch well out into the suburbs, and even to outlying cities such as Uijongbu and Inch'on. The stations are well designed, with maps and information in English. They are often also linked to the underground shopping arcades that are such a feature of Korean cities. As in other cities, the subways can become very crowded at the morning and evening rush hours; the wise traveler avoids such times! They can also be very full in the late evenings, as the businessmen (and a few women) make their way home. This is a time to be careful. Just occasionally, a drunken passenger may take exception to a foreigner, especially if the latter is a man with a Korean woman, or a woman who appears to be Korean. In recent years, there have been anti-American outbursts on the subways in the evenings. It is best not to talk too loudly or to draw attention to oneself.

Taxis

South Korean cities are well supplied with taxis. In Seoul, these come in a variety of styles and prices; the bigger and cleaner the car, the more expensive it will be, and the more likely it will be to have a driver who understands some English and who will charge the correct fare. It is a good idea to have destinations written out by a Korean, since foreigners' pronunciation is often difficult for Koreans to understand.

Walking

While there are parts of all South Korean cities that are pleasant to explore on foot, such as market areas, and in Seoul the historic center, most cities are not particularly good for walking. There are few historic buildings and the general quality of architecture is not high, although there are some exceptions. Amenities such as public toilets used to be rare, but, especially in Seoul, availability has much improved as a result of a series of international events beginning with the 1986 Asian Games. These events have also led to improvements in facilities to help the disabled.

Those on foot need to be careful late at night in certain areas. Physical violence against foreigners is still rare, but as with the subway system, late night drunks, however apparently respectable, can be abusive. Whatever the temptation, it is probably best for a foreigner to keep out of Korean quarrels.

Walking and hiking are possible, especially in the mountains. These are everywhere; even Seoul has mountains within the city boundaries. Intensive agriculture can hinder the walker in the countryside, and one must be very careful not to damage the dykes around the paddy fields. Seoul has its cross-country running clubs, including the Hash House Harriers, who welcome newcomers.

GETTING AROUND IN THE NORTH

Most travelers to North Korea arrive at Pyongyang's International Airport, Sunan, just outside the city. The only regular carrier is the national airline, Air Koryo, which flies to Beijing twice a week, and also serves Shenyang in northeast China and the Russian Far East. The other main route is by rail from China. The journey takes about twenty hours to or from Beijing, but travelers should be aware that the train can often be delayed, especially in the summer rainy season. The third permitted route is across the Tumen River to the special economic zone at Rajin-Sonbong, in the far northeast of the country. It is not easy to get to Pyongyang.

All visitors to North Korea need to be hosted by a local organization, either Korean or foreign. For tourists, this will be the (North) Korean National Travel Organization. Visitors also need a visa. This, except in very rare circumstances, must be obtained outside the country. Most people use the DPRK Embassy in Beijing (near Ritan Park in the east of the city), but if there is a DPRK Embassy in your country, you can get a visa there. It is wise to allow at least a month and probably longer to obtain your visa. Prospective visitors should note that tourist visas are not normally issued for visitors from Japan and the United States. The cost of visas varies. The North Koreans argue that they charge visitors on a scale relating to what North Koreans are charged. So if your country charges $30, a North Korean visa will cost you $30. In practice, the rates charged seem to vary from this rule somewhat. On departures by air you will have to pay a tax.

For the present, cell phones are taken away on entry into North Korea, and in any case, they do not work except right up close to the Chinese border. If you can, leave yours elsewhere. If you must bring it, on arrival be prepared to see it put into a little numbered bag. You will be given a ticket and will be able to claim the phone back on departure. It is probably best also to avoid bringing in publications in Korean and those relating to North Korea. The North Koreans are generally not happy with much that is written about their country, and may confiscate material relating to the peninsula. You will be expected to fill out a customs form listing valuables and currency.

All visitors will be met; there are no taxis or other transportation facilities at the airport. Most visitors will have a Korean host waiting for them. Those joining or visiting embassies and international organizations will be met by representatives from those bodies. Do not panic if there appears to be nobody to greet you at first. They will arrive, but sometimes have trouble fighting their way through the waiting crowds. Nobody has ever been left completely unattended! The airport can be a bit daunting as people struggle to get themselves and their luggage through the checkpoints. It is probably best to relax and let things take their course. Luggage is rarely lost or left behind, but the airport staff may stack it up in a system known only to them. So, if something appears to have gone missing, ask your hosts to search thoroughly before panicking.

Once within North Korea, foreigners with Korean hosts are likely to find that they are kept on a very tight rein. Those responsible for you take their duties very seriously and will often refuse to let you out of their sight. International driver's licenses are not accepted and there are no facilities for self-drive cars. Only resident foreigners who have taken a local driving test can drive; heads of international organizations and diplomatic missions are exempt from taking the test as long as they can produce a valid driver's license. There are rental cars outside hotels and some shops, recognized by the number "50" on their license plates. However, unless a Korean accompanies you, these may well refuse to take you.

All travel will be arranged. Because the railways are in a poor state as a result of lack of maintenance and general economic decline, journey times are long and unpredictable. The condition of the rolling stock is also poor. Most journeys, therefore, are done by road. Cars provided are likely to be a 1960s or 1970s vintage Volvo or Mercedes-Benz, though there are a few modern Toyota Landcruisers also available. All vehicles are poorly maintained—tires, in particular, are often very worn down—but the drivers do their best. One hazard is that many taxi drivers seem to drink. Refuse to go with a driver who has been drinking. In theory, it is illegal to drink and drive in North Korea, but most North Korean drivers seem blissfully unaware of this.

There are no intercity buses. Within most major cities there are buses, but foreigners are generally not taken on (or perhaps even allowed on) them. The same is true of the trams/light railways found in some cities, and of Pyongyang's extensive fleet of trams, buses, and trolleybuses. Foreigners do occasionally break the taboo, however. Pyongyang has a two-line subway system. Foreigners usually visit this as a tourist attraction rather than a means of transportation, though in theory it is open for use.

Walking around is often discouraged. Until recently, even resident foreigners outside Pyongyang (and in the early days of international aid, even within Pyongyang) were confined to hotels. Today resident foreigners and their guests usually have no problem. Resident foreigners may also use bicycles, but there are none available to rent.

Foreigners do go jogging in Pyongyang. Away from the cities, there is good hiking in the many mountain areas, but visitors are likely to be closely monitored and are unlikely to be allowed to go off on their own. Resident foreigners are in theory somewhat freer, but even they find that there are limits on where they can go.

WINTER DRIVING

Finally, a note of caution on winter driving that applies to both North and South Korea. Winter driving can be dangerous. Snow and ice turn many roads into ice rinks. In some parts of South Korea, snow tires and chains may be required. The watchword must be care, but not all Korean drivers seem to be aware of the dangers, and sometimes drive too fast on icy roads.

In North Korea, it is the poor condition of the vehicles, combined with untreated roads, which poses the biggest danger. Do not hesitate to ask for drivers to go more slowly.

WHERE TO STAY IN THE SOUTH
Hotels

You will find that South Korea is very well served for hotel accommodation. The official ratings system lists hotels as super deluxe (SDL), deluxe (DL), first, second, and third class, but these categories, according to the Korean National Tourist Organization (KNTO), do not necessarily correspond to the classifications used in Western countries.

In Seoul and the other major cities there are many world-class hotels; they also come with world-class prices, and some are members of international chains. They have all the facilities and the standard of service you would expect from such a type of hotel; swimming pools, jogging paths, and high-class restaurants. The restaurants will include at least one Western restaurant, usually with a French-sounding name, Chinese and Japanese restaurants, and of course, a Korean restaurant. The rooms will be well appointed, with international television, access points for computers, and mini-bars. The latter can be very expensive. Robes and slippers are invariably provided. Once, razors, toothbrushes, and other toiletries might also have been available, but this is less likely nowadays, since the South Korean government has decreed that these are an unnecessary luxury. If you find yourself without a toothbrush, however, most hotels will happily provide one. Many hotels can be booked from abroad, via travel agents or through the Internet.

All such hotels will have a coffee shop, which serves simple meals and is often open both earlier and later than the standard restaurants, and any number of bars. "Irish" bars are enjoying a vogue in Seoul, just as in other parts of the world. Several of these hotels have special club floors as well, which, in addition to providing such business services as fax, Internet, and similar resources, will often have a private bar with a free "happy hour" period for drinks.

In the big cities, such hotels are good places to eat, to meet people—most Koreans are very happy to meet and be seen in the major hotels—and even to do some modest shopping. If you cannot manage without a particular Western brand of toothpaste, for example, there is a chance that you will find it in such a place. Most have small bookshops and other more general outlets. Sometimes, the bookshops will turn up long-out-of-print works hard to find anywhere else. In Seoul, many of the central high-class hotels link up with the extensive network of underground shopping centers. These central hotels are also good venues from which to watch Koreans. They are often the choice for introducing young couples to each other, for example.

"Tourist Hotels"

If you wish to be more adventurous, you should try some of the smaller and cheaper hotels. These are often described as "tourist hotels." They will have more simple facilities, but will usually have a Korean and a Chinese restaurant, and perhaps a coffee shop. The bars are likely to be brighter and brasher than the dark lounges of the more expensive places. Especially away from Seoul, they will often offer good value for money, and in some places they will be all that is available. The staff will be less sophisticated than in the international-class hotels but will usually be helpful and certainly friendly. Although simpler, there is no reason why small hotels should be any less comfortable than their more expensive counterparts.

"*Yogwan*"

Even more modest are *yogwan*, or Korean inns. The Chinese characters read the same as the Japanese *ryokan*, and mean simply "building for travelers." In practice, few Korean *yogwan* equate to the *ryokan*, either in style of building or standard of comfort. Only in the remoter islands or in some mountain areas is the visitor likely to come across a *yogwan* that is anything more than a concrete shell—but they can still be fun to stay in. Remember that in most *yogwan*, the price includes at least dinner and breakfast—though do not be surprised if, away from the big cities, these two meals are more or less the same!

Sleeping arrangements vary in the *yogwan*. In some you will find a few rooms with Western-style beds; in others, you will sleep on the floor, Korean-style. In the latter case, there will be a mattress and a thick quilt, plus sheets. Whether you sleep on the floor or on a bed, you may find the traditional Korean pillows literally rather hard to take. Once they would have been wood or porcelain, but even today, they are hard. There is usually no rule about how many people stay in a Korean-style room. Just make it clear on checking in. Also remember that, as in a Korean house, shoes are not worn indoors.

Another thing to check is the standard of cleanliness. You will have no problems in top-class establishments, which are invariably spotless, but the same standards may not apply in more remote areas. Do not hesitate to ask for a room to be cleaned, or for clean sheets and pillowcases, if you suspect that those offered you have been used before.

Youth Hostels

For travelers with very limited budgets, South Korea has some fifty-five youth hostels, all of which belong to the Korea Youth Hostel Association (KYHA). These hostels will be found in the major cities as well as in scenic areas. Visitors who are used to the relatively small-scale hostels of Europe are likely to be in for a surprise. The smallest has over a hundred beds, while there are several very large ones with a thousand beds or more. Membership is required, though membership of a foreign YHA may be accepted. In order to guarantee a place, bookings should be made in advance.

Home Stays

Home visits are a possibility in South Korea, although, except in the country, you are increasingly unlikely to stay in traditional Korean housing; it is much more probable that you will find yourself in one of the much-sought-after modern apartment blocks. The apartments have modern facilities, including toilets, baths, and central heating, and are much more secure than low-rise houses. As has been mentioned, some of the rules of traditional houses still apply within the modern apartment—you do not wear shoes, of course. Slippers will be provided, and you change these for a different set of slippers when using the toilet. Although the old division into men's and women's quarters is not possible in a modern apartment, it is sometimes quite rare to see the wife in such a home. She will be busy in the kitchen, even if there are staff to help prepare food, and may not even eat with the guests on whose behalf she has labored. For the foreign visitor, a home stay will provide a good introduction to Korean life. If you get the opportunity to stay in a traditional house, take it! As is often the case in all types of Korean homes, life will be lived at floor level. In winter, the house will be heated by the under-floor system known as *ondol*. The hot gases from the kitchen fire are drawn under the floor to a chimney at the other side of the house. Floors can sometimes become very warm, which is fine on a snowy winter's morning, but can be a bit overpowering as winter gives way to spring. If you are staying in a remote area in a traditional house or inn with *ondol*, make sure that a window is open or that there is some other means of ventilation. Each year, carbon monoxide poisoning kills a few people because they have slept in tightly sealed rooms into which the gas has come though an undetected crack in the floor.

Temples

For those who prefer something even more unusual, it may be possible to stay in a Buddhist temple. Because Buddhism was forced out of the cities during the long Yi dynasty (1392–1910), temples that survived tended to be in more remote, mountainous areas. Today, these are often prime tourist destinations, and so in recent years, some temples have been taking in visitors for short stays, to experience, however briefly, the life of contemplation and ceremony practiced by the monks. There are also a number of temples that have traditionally accepted foreigners for greater or lesser periods. Such attachments involve following the full ascetic training of the monks, which can be quite a shock to participants from the West.

Longer Term

Longer-stay visitors, or even those taking up residence, might like to consider using a residence hotel, of which there are several in Seoul. Essentially these are fully furnished service apartments, sometimes attached to hotels. They will provide health club facilities, restaurants, and other requirements, such as Internet access, but will also provide amenities, such as a kitchen, to allow one to lead a more independent life.

WHERE TO STAY IN THE NORTH

Accommodation in North Korea offers much less choice. Pyongyang has a selection of hotels where foreign visitors are lodged, but in most other places that foreigners are able to visit, there is one hotel and that is that. The one exception is Kaesong, the former capital of the Koryo kingdom (918–1392). Kaesong has a considerable amount of charm, mainly because a large number of traditional houses have survived, since the city was not bombed during the Korean War. Today there are two hotels. One is a modern block, best avoided. The other is delightful, being made up of a series of old houses with small courtyards, traditional rooms, and modern facilities. If the opportunity arises, this is a good place to stay, and it has some of the best food in North Korea.

Pyongyang's hotels range from the supposedly deluxe Koryo and Yanggakdo Hotels to some very simple places, including one that is called a youth hostel. The prices are relatively high and the quality of service has been low, but there are signs of improvement since the 2002 economic reforms. A major change in Pyongyang's hotels is the increasing availability of international satellite television, but there are other positive developments as well. At one time, the Koryo Hotel rooms could not be locked, for example, but this has now changed. Cleanliness can also be a problem, as can supplies of hot water. In hotels away from Pyongyang, the latter is usually limited to short periods in the morning and evening.

Various government ministries also have guesthouses for senior foreign visitors. These are likely to be more attractive places to stay than the hotels, since they are often set in gardens or other pleasant surroundings, but they suffer from two main disadvantages: they are sometimes remote from the city center, and they are guarded—so much so that visitors often find that they cannot leave the grounds. Visitors should be warned that, while bedrooms will be kept warm in winter, public areas, including restaurants, are often not heated at all. This can be something of a shock in January and February.

HEALTH
The South

Standards of health care are high in South Korea. There are excellent, if expensive, hospitals, available in all major cities. Many physicians and dental surgeons have trained abroad, often in the United States. Western-style medicinal drugs are readily available and in regular use. Some foreigners have found that South Korean doctors have a tendency to overprescribe. The sensible visitor will make sure that he or she has adequate supplies of any medical needs, as well as insurance. Water is generally safe, and bottled water is widely available for those who prefer it. Cholera, once common, is now rare, as are malaria and encephalitis. However, since malaria has reappeared in North Korea, it is wise to take precautions against mosquito bites. Avoid uncooked food, and be cautious about hotel buffets; food may often sit around for a long time.

The North

The visitor to North Korea should be aware that health care is now somewhat precarious. Many North Korean physicians have been well trained either in North Korea, Eastern Europe, or the former Soviet Union. But lack of funds and ideological differences mean that most of that training would have taken place a long time ago, so North Korean doctors today will be unfamiliar with current practices. Many conditions such as malaria, once eradicated, have come back in recent years. This will not affect visitors to the main cities, but anyone going further into the countryside should be aware of the problem.

In addition, the economic decline of recent years has hit the health service badly. Few hospitals, even in Pyongyang, have up-to-date equipment, and most lack facilities such as X-ray machines, general anesthetics, and drugs. North Koreans are helpful when there is a problem, but in general, any medical or dental emergency will involve a speedy departure from the DPRK.

Tap water is not safe. Use bottled water wherever possible and avoid uncooked food. Bring an adequate supply of prescription drugs and common medicines such as aspirin. The latter may sometimes be available, but there is no guarantee—and in any case, the product may come from Russia, China, or Eastern Europe, and may not be easily identifiable.

chapter eight

BUSINESS BRIEFING

The rapid transformation of the South Korean economy, from poverty in the 1950s to the world's eleventh largest in the 1990s, has meant that more and more foreigners do business with the country. In many ways, this proves no more difficult than doing business anywhere else. Your Korean counterparts are likely to be as well-educated and experienced as you are— many South Koreans have studied in Europe and North America, and some will have lived abroad. The first generation of Korea's business leaders, the heads of the *chaebol*, or industrial conglomerates, may not have had much exposure to the outside world in their youth, but their successors will be sophisticated and experienced. This is less the case in the North, but even there more exposure to the outside world is beginning to change attitudes and style. Nevertheless, the Koreans do some things slightly differently from businesses in the West. If you have negotiated in China or Japan, you will soon recognize a kinship with the Koreans.

CONFUCIAN VALUES

Some describe these common characteristics as "Confucian," but, as one academic writer has noted, the trouble with "Confucianism" is that it is as full of contradictions as any other set of beliefs that have developed over long periods of time and in very different environments. A complicating factor is that the Confucian canon actually put the merchant in a low position in the hierarchy, which does not square with the respect paid to successful businessmen in Korea today. While the behavior of some South Korean modern industrialists may correspond to these precepts, that of others does not.

That said, you will hear the term "Confucianism" used to describe Korean business practices. This tends to mean that Koreans value hierarchy, with age receiving more respect than youth, prefer order to chaos, have a high regard for education, dislike ostentation, and emphasize the group rather than the individual. It also includes a belief in the value of hard work; the last year or so has seen much soul-searching in South Korea as some occupations have moved from a five-and-a-half- or six-day working week to a five-day week. Now the newspapers are full of articles on how to use the extra time profitably—staying in bed is not seen as an option!

WOMEN IN BUSINESS

Another aspect of Confucianism that has undoubtedly affected Korea is the attitude toward women. Women ranked low in the Confucian hierarchy, and such attitudes are taking a long time to change. Korean women are fighting against such discrimination, and are increasingly making their presence felt in areas traditionally dominated by men. But they have a long way to go, and do not yet occupy many senior positions in business or industry. Non-Korean women benefit from being outsiders to whom the normal rules do not apply, but they may well feel that they are not being treated as the equals of their male counterparts.

FACE

Then there is "face." This is almost as hard to define as Confucianism itself. In some ways, it boils down to avoiding doing or saying something that will embarrass your Korean counterpart in front of others. Remember that it is not only the person who is embarrassed who loses "face." The person perpetuating the deed has also lost "face," because they have put somebody else in an impossible position. The way to handle difficult situations is to avoid direct confrontation or blame in front of others, and then to tackle the issue in private. So, do not tell a person that he or she is lying, even if you know that to be the case. Take them aside and explain that your understanding of the position is different from theirs. This allows both of you to move around the problem, and, with luck, to find a solution.

This same principle applies to business negotiations. Try always to avoid being negative, and never rule anything out. A soft answer can often produce a solution; the other side does not want you to lose face either.

It follows that anger, or the appearance of anger, should be avoided as far as possible. The Confucian gentleman does not get angry.

Business gifts are also a matter of face. As in Japan, the giving and receiving of presents is a very important part of social behavior. Gifts are expected as a means of showing sincerity. Give the right present, and you have shown that you understand the position of the recipient. This is not so much a matter of expense as of quality and appropriateness. If you are not sure, consult a Korean.

FORMALITY

The Korean approach to business is more formal than is now customary in the West. Those engaged in business should dress the part; dressing down is not a Korean characteristic. Jackets may well remain on, even if the temperatures are high. Set-piece negotiations are common, with large groups on either side of the table. Normally, however, only the principals on each side will speak. The others are there for consultations if necessary, and perhaps to give advice in writing as the meeting progresses. Koreans will not be impressed if junior members of a team intervene unbidden.

This formality may sometimes spill over into social occasions associated with business. At a cocktail party, do not expect older people to talk to younger ones, and do not be surprised if it is hard to get much out of junior members on the Korean side. Sometimes the alcohol invariably consumed on such occasions will break down the barriers, but not always, especially if the

Korean host is particularly senior. If you are invited to a bar, however, then the atmosphere will be more relaxed, and the consumption of alcohol even higher!

BUSINESS DRESS SENSE

Koreans tend to dress formally during the working week. This applies to North and South, and to both men and women. Men will generally wear somber-colored Western suits. There are some exceptions, especially in South Korea. Among academics, for instance, it is not unusual to find sports jackets, though usually of a fairly conservative style and color. An artist may wear a French-style beret, and have a beard. In some of the bigger Korean companies, all staff, whether managerial or shop-floor workers, will wear the company uniform. During the hottest period in summer, some of this formality may be relaxed, and open-necked shirts will become the norm in government offices. If in doubt, however, a man should wear a tie.

Women will find that their Korean counterparts will dress conservatively. Bare shoulders are not acceptable, and short skirts are strictly for the young. Trousers and trouser suits are very popular among South Korean women, and a well-tailored pair of trousers will prove suitable dress for most occasions. This style is equally appropriate in North Korea, though especially in Pyongyang, women will tend to wear skirts from about mid-March to mid-November.

Foreigners do not have to conform exactly to Korean standards, but for those doing business, it is wise not to get out of line with Korean practice. Loud sports shirts and shorts are not acceptable for the office, or for formal calls, even in the hottest and stickiest weather.

Wearing clothes appropriate for the occasion is a mark of discernment. Koreans take leisure as seriously as work. If you are invited to play golf or tennis, therefore, it is important that you dress correctly. Even picnics and mountain climbing demand the right outfit. No matter that numerous Koreans wearing quite the wrong shoes and clothes for going up Korean mountains will pass you; the real gentleman (and lady) will have good stout shoes, a proper hat, and a stout stick. Again, Koreans will appreciate it if you have made the effort. In any case, such equipment makes sense on the surprisingly rugged hills of Korea. Low they may be, but easy they are not!

INTRODUCTIONS

When introduced, you should bend your upper body slightly. Koreans generally bow sparingly, unlike the Japanese. Among men, you should also offer your hand. There are no hard and fast rules about who should offer a hand first. If two Koreans meet, the senior will generally make the first move, but the same rules do not apply to foreigners. It is less common for Korean women to shake hands.

THE BUSINESS CARD

After the introduction, you should present your business card. Business cards are extensively used in both North and South Korea, and it is a good idea to have some even if you are only staying for a short while. You can of course have them printed at home, but there are advantages in waiting until you arrive in Korea. They can be prepared quickly, and Korean printers will add your name and address, or that of your company or organization, in Korean. Cards should be offered with both hands if possible, or, if that is not possible, with the right hand. When receiving a card, it is good form to study it a little before putting it away. One useful purchase to make while in Korea is a small wallet, usually leather or eel-skin, in which to store both your own cards and those that you have collected. Another is a book to which you can transfer cards as your collection grows. South Korean business cards are often very informative, with details of cell phones and e-mail, and picture cards are increasingly common. North Korean cards, by contrast, are usually pretty minimalist in the information that they convey: name, title, organization, and address, with a general telephone number, and possibly a fax number, for the organization. It is very difficult to obtain an individual number.

Because they attach importance to their own hierarchies, Koreans will also be interested in yours. Here the business card is very important, and it is a great mistake to try to operate without one. Put as much information as you can on yours, and be warned: there is a growing practice in South Korea of putting photographs on cards. Koreans will eagerly seize on your business card, as it will, they hope, supply them with some clues about you and your status. Educational qualifications impress, especially if they come from a well-known establishment. Ranks and titles are also important, so if you can, add these to your business cards. In addition to what they can learn from your card, Koreans may well make detailed inquiries about your background, education, and beliefs. This is to be able to place you, to see where you might fit into their system.

Anything that seems confrontational should be

avoided. Koreans tend to avoid too much eye contact. It is therefore regarded as somewhat rude to look straight into another person's eyes all the time while conversing. Koreans fix their gaze between the eyes and the nose of the other person and will often glance downwards. Failure to "look somebody in the eye" is not considered a sign of weakness in Korea. Neither is it necessary to provide a "firm" handshake. Just a touch will do.

PREPARATION

As with anywhere else, to conduct business successfully in Korea requires a certain amount of forethought and planning. Read and study as much as you can in advance of beginning your efforts—such preparation is never wasted. Be patient, and do not expect speedy results. While contemporary South Korea often seems a place of great hustle and bustle, possessed of a "can-do" attitude, and in the North you may be pushed for a quick decision, there is an older Korean tradition of not doing things in a hurry, and it is wise to bear this in mind.

You should also be sure of what you want from your link with a Korean company, and establish which companies might meet these needs. As far as South Korea is concerned, there is now a large amount of literature about Korean companies

available, both in print and electronic form.
Information can also be gleaned from Chambers
of Commerce and both South Korean and foreign
embassies. The South Korean business scene is
somewhat more complicated than it was before
the 1997 economic crisis. The crisis led to the
breakup of the *chaebol*, or conglomerates, into
separate companies. The initial confusion has
now settled down, but changes that have occurred
mean that you may need to consider a wider
group than you might have done before 1997.

Perseverance

An essential element to conducting business in
Korea is perseverance, both in presenting your
case and in keeping up contacts with your Korean
counterpart. Do not expect to conclude most
business transactions in a single session. This may
sometimes happen, but it is the exception. Rather,
be prepared at the outset for a long haul. Expect
to return to Korea more than once if your
business involves any form of long-term
commitment. By doing so, you show sincerity.

NEGOTIATIONS

When in Korea, negotiate as the Koreans do.
One person, preferably the most senior, should
carry out the negotiations. Any others are

there to advise (ideally in writing), not to join in the discussion.

Actual negotiations are likely to take time, with formal presentations being the order of the day. Remember to allow time for interpretation. Many Koreans will not be at ease with spoken English, even if they can read it. Besides, interpretation allows both sides time to think. Do not address your remarks to  the interpreter, however. Instead, while not staring directly at him or her, make sure that you keep your eyes toward your counterpart. Use titles such as chairman or president instead of names alone; "Chairman Kim" is better than "Mr. Kim." Do not suggest the use of given names. Koreans rarely do so among themselves, and the chances are that you will end up being addressed as "Mr. John" or "Madam Sarah," which perhaps does not convey the message you wish to get across.

Do not give all your points away at the beginning. Ideally, the foreign side should have its own dedicated interpreter(s) to make sure that its case is really put across. In some cases a native Korean speaker may tend to empathize with the Korean side rather than your own. Fortunately, this is not always the case, and it is also becoming easier to employ a nonnative speaker as more institutions teach Korean to a high standard.

It is much better to let concessions or additional offers come out in the course of negotiations—that way, they seem more of a gain for the other side. Be less worried about reaching an agreed-upon document than about getting a broad and acceptable base on which to keep in contact. Contracts, even when signed, are not necessarily seen as the final word, but merely a stage, albeit a more definite stage, on the road to final agreement. If you cannot reach final agreement, make every effort to avoid a hostile break. If goodwill remains, it may be possible to come back to an issue after it has been reviewed.

Negotiations may go on late. Koreans generally work long hours, and do not expect to go home at the end of the formal working day. On some evenings, there may be formal dinners (you should reciprocate any such hospitality), followed by drinking and possibly singing. You can excuse yourself from drinking on health or religious grounds, but somebody on your side should be able to keep up with the Korean side.

It is best to avoid being humorous; jokes that need to go through an interpreter tend to fall flat, however good the joke or the interpreter. Remember also that Korean laughter will not always be related to humor; Koreans often laugh to hide embarrassment or to soften bad news, so be careful how you interpret their actions.

BUSINESS ENTERTAINMENT

As well as formal dinners, which are usually held in upmarket restaurants, the Koreans also go in for informal post-work, or post-dinner, entertainment. This involves more food and very macho drinking rounds. *Poktanjoo* is a way of mixing whiskey and beer, and downing it in one go.

At the apex of the entertaining world in South Korea are *kisaeng* houses, where well-trained women entertain customers. Like the *geisha* tradition in Japan, it derives from the Confucian idea that it is the duty of women to serve men in all things. Dinner in a *kisaeng* house, along with the subsequent drinking games, is an expensive undertaking, and foreigners are likely to find that invitations to such establishments are rare.

The *Kisaeng* Party

A typical *kisaeng* evening will involve much food and drink, with the girls (sometimes mature women) feeding their male companions and playing party games with them. There is also likely to be singing and dancing. Sometimes the entertainment is confined to traditional-style performances by the *kisaeng*, but nowadays the rest of the party are also likely to join in, in the style of a karaoke bar. While it is not unknown for a foreigner to organize a *kisaeng* party, it is wise to be guided by a Korean before attempting this.

Rare Entertainment

Visiting the South Korean city of Kwangju, I took part in my only *kisaeng* party. As the evening progressed, the young lady looking after me, in addition to massaging my legs from time to time to an alarmingly high point on my thighs, kept offering me pieces of raw octopus that were still moving. I declined both the continuation of the massage and the octopus. Eventually, however, after a couple of hours, the octopus appeared not to be moving and so, when she picked up a piece with suckers on her chopsticks, I took it. It promptly grabbed the side of my mouth. Eventually I pried it off and swallowed it. My foreign colleague, a biologist by training, maintained that since it responded to stimuli and appeared to have the ability to move, it was alive.

Below the *kisaeng* house there are a variety of other establishments. "Salons" or cocktail lounges will provide the female accompaniment in less exalted surroundings than the *kisaeng* house, but can also be expensive. Salons may also be called "business clubs," but the service is the same. In all these establishments, if the chemistry and the cost is right, it may be possible to move on to more personal relations. But be warned, it is not part of the service as such.

Karaoke

Most popular of all are karaoke bars. Karaoke has become a term so widely used in Korea that it can be considered part of the language. At a karaoke bar or room—the terms seem interchangeable—everybody in the party will be expected to sing, so the wise foreign visitor has a few songs prepared, whatever the state of his or (more rarely) her singing voice. Singing is so popular and widespread that you will encounter it on many other occasions as well. In good weather, many foreigners, even on short visits, find that they are invited to company or organization picnics, and these too provide an excuse for singing.

And visitors to North Korea need not think that they will escape. There are several karaoke establishments in Pyongyang and even run-down provincial hotels may have a karaoke room. The custom of calling for songs after dinner is well established among the ministries too, so however formal the diplomatic occasion, or the negotiations with the trade ministry, you are likely to be called on to sing in Pyongyang. And do not worry—however good or bad you are, there will certainly be a demand for an encore!

GIFTS

Presents in the business context may be much larger than those given in the course of ordinary social contacts. Usually there will be a reciprocal exchange, which at least keeps the balance. Sometimes, however, the gift offered and the gift expected may be quite different. Perhaps the most sensible policy to follow is never to give more than you are happy with, whatever the hints and pressures from the other side.

THE NORTH

Most of the above applies to South Korea, but much of it is also applicable to dealings with North Korea. The North may formally deny that it is a Confucian society but many "Confucian" traits still prevail, whether as respect for hierarchy or in attitudes toward women. In the North, entertainment may be less lavish and probably will not go on so long. However, it will form part of the business of doing business, as will the ability to match toast for toast and song for song. Gift giving, too, is important, although it is not always reciprocal. Again, you will find that the person who is clearly willing to remain engaged will be likely to succeed—"old friends" are valued. Be warned that contracts are even more likely to be seen as but a stage in a process in the North.

In North Korea, people will be less familiar with Western ways than their counterparts in the South. Expectations can sometimes be very much out of line with reality. There is sometimes a tendency in North Korea to see things as a right rather than a possibility. North Korean negotiators can be very tough and demanding, and sometimes come across as very intimidating. The sense of isolation that many foreigners feel, cut off from sources of information and often kept apart from other foreigners, adds to the sense of intimidation, but firmness usually pays off.

There are many companies and individuals who have had business dealings with North Korea that have met both sides' needs. Be honest but careful, and make sure that a substantial portion of your payment comes before the completion of a deal, and you should be successful.

chapter nine

COMMUNICATING

LANGUAGE

Just under 70 million people in the world speak
Korean. The vast majority are on the Korean
peninsula, but there are about 2.15 million in the
U.S.A., 2.14 million in China, 640,000 in Japan,
and 500,00 in the former Soviet Union. Although
there were many people of Korean ethnic origin
in the Soviet Union, the language suffered badly
during Stalin's time, and few now speak it.
Outside these areas, Korean has not enjoyed the
popularity of Chinese or Japanese, and relatively
few non-Koreans know the language.

Most Westerners find Korean a difficult
language. To the complexity of the grammar are
added a number of other factors that cause
problems. Korean has absorbed many words of
Chinese origin, which exist alongside native
Korean words—both must be learned. Korean is a
language with many levels of speech, with
numerous honorifics depending on who is
addressing whom, and in what context; there are
at least nine degrees of respect or familiarity. In

South Korea, a visitor who speaks some Korean will come in for much praise—only when one's language skills are really good will this praise disappear! In North Korea, while a little knowledge of Korean will earn similar plaudits, evidence of real language skills will be looked upon with suspicion, at least at first. Korean-speaking foreigners are seen as potential spies and are not welcome.

Although all Koreans can communicate with each other, there are several distinct dialects. The political divide has led to each side stressing that "correct" speech is based around that of either Seoul or Pyongyang. Kim Il Sung condemned Seoul speech in the 1960s as being "firmly rooted in the rotten bourgeois life" of the past, full of loan words from Chinese, Japanese, and English, and overly feminine. In the South, North Korean speech is criticized for its heavy ideological content and for a deliberate break with the peninsula's past by stripping out Chinese-derived words. South Korea has a heavy influx of English-derived words as a result of a strong American presence since 1945, although even in the North, words such as camera, television, and hotel are in common use. It is possible that the influx of foreign words also affects the generations in South Korea; as elsewhere, older people profess themselves unable to understand the young. The latter pride themselves on being up to date in the "cool" language of international pop music and fashion.

The Korean Alphabet

The written language as used in South Korea requires some knowledge of Chinese characters as well as of the Korean alphabet. In North Korea Chinese characters are no longer in use, though they can sometimes still be seen at historical sites or monuments. Kim Il Sung seems to have been proud of his Chinese calligraphy and wrote a number of inscriptions for buildings or places that he had caused to be restored.

The Korean alphabet is known as *Han'gul* in South Korea, and as *Choson muncha* in the North, and dates from the reign of King Sejong in the fifteenth century. In order to provide a means of writing more attuned to Korean grammar than Chinese ideographs, and also one that would be more generally accessible, he set teams of scholars to work on devising a new method of writing.

Today, all Koreans, North and South, are very proud of what they usually describe as the most scientific alphabet in the world, sometimes extending this to the language itself. The alphabet is simple to learn; an afternoon's assiduous work is all that is required to learn the individual letters, though much more is needed to be able to combine them properly, and to be aware of the subtle changes that take place in such combinations. Acquisition of the alphabet can help in traveling, since in some remote parts, romanized signs may be in short supply. It is also nice to be able to read slogans, even if they turn out to be saying no more than "Drink Coca-Cola"!

Vowels	ㅏ	ㅑ	ㅓ	ㅕ	ㅗ	ㅛ	ㅜ	ㅠ	ㅡ	ㅣ
	a	ya	ŏ	yŏ	o	yo	u	yu	ŭ	i

Consonants	ㄱ	ㄴ	ㄷ	ㄹ	ㅁ	ㅂ	ㅅ
	k, g	n	t, d	r, l	m	p, b	s, sh

	ㅇ	ㅈ	ㅊ	ㅋ	ㅌ	ㅍ	ㅎ
		ch, j	ch' k'	k'	t'	p'	h

안녕하세요 (How do you do?)

an nyŏng ha se yo

There are a few traps for the foreigner. One is the "r" and "l" sounds, which, as in Japanese and Chinese, are almost interchangeable. There are also some differences in pronunciation between the northern and southern halves of the country—these have nothing to do with politics, however, and long predate the division of the peninsula. Thus, as already mentioned, the surname "Lee," "Li," "I," or "Yi," used in the south, is usually found as "Ree," "Rhee," or "Ri" in the north. Do not worry too much; Koreans will recognize it whichever way you pronounce it.

The language bears some similarity to those of neighboring countries. There are no definite or indefinite articles, grammatical number, or gender distinctions. Pronouns are rarely used, and sentences are often vague about the subject and tense of a verb. At the same time, while Korean contains many Chinese words, its grammar is very different. The grammar of Korean and Japanese is very similar, but the two languages sound very different. Korean appears to be linked to the Altaic group of languages, which includes Mongolian, Manchu, Hungarian, and Finnish, to name a few, but there is no clear evidence of any historical link between most of the languages so described. Certainly, if you speak Finnish or Hungarian, you will not find many opportunities to do so in Korea!

Transliteration

How to romanize Korean has been a problem for Westerners since they first encountered the language in the seventeenth century. For a long time, French influence was strongest as a result of the nineteenth-century French Roman Catholic missionaries who worked (and in many cases, suffered martyrdom) in Korea.

Two Americans devised the most widely used system of romanization in the late 1930s. George McAfee McCune (1908–48) was born in

Pyongyang of missionary parents, while Edwin Oldfather Reischauer (1910–90) was a scholar of Japanese and later U.S. ambassador to Japan. Working together with a group of Korean scholars, they created the McCune-Reischauer System, which was published by the Royal Asiatic Society Korea Branch in 1939. This system aimed to be a phonetic translation of modern Korean, using English consonants and Italian vowels, rather than a literal transcription of *han'gul*. Its use spread rapidly, and it has become the most favored way of romanizing Korean. It has been used in South Korea from time to time, and, in a modified (and unacknowledged) version, it is still used in North Korea. Other systems in use include the Yale system, devised in the 1950s, which is much favored by linguists.

Many Koreans do not like the McCune-Reischauer System, however, since it does not exactly represent *han'gul*. Some Koreans appear to object because foreigners devised it, and others have seen it as tainted by links with Japan, because of Reischauer's involvement. In South Korea, various attempts have been made to develop a more acceptable system, the latest of which was introduced in 2000, ousting McCune-Reischauer from all official publications, road signs, and similar material. Many English speakers do not like the new system because it throws up

unfamiliar and unsightly combinations of letters,
and can also lead to as many mispronunciations
as McCune-Reischauer—the surname "Pak"
(Park), for example, becomes "Bag"; "*tongnip*,"
independence, becomes "*dogrib*"; and the province
of Cholla bukdo, "*Jeollabuk-do*." No doubt, in
time, it will all become as familiar as McCune-
Reischauer, but it is a pity that romanization, one
of the few points on which North and South have
shared the same position, at least in recent years,
has become another dividing point.

FACE-TO-FACE

Communicating will generally not be too much of
a problem, at least at a simple level. Koreans both
North and South learn English from their
schooldays onward, so in theory English is the
most widespread second language on the
peninsula—as French is in Britain! Remember that
many Koreans never have the chance to use their
foreign languages with native speakers, so they may
well be shy of trying to talk to you. Persevere and
your efforts may be rewarded. If you are not having
much luck with the spoken language, try writing
things down. Many people can read English even if
they are nervous about speaking it.

If you have other languages, it may be worth
trying them. Very old Koreans may still have some

Japanese, for example, and most South Koreans will understand some written Chinese, since Chinese characters are still in use for some purposes. German and French will sometimes yield results. If all else fails, sign language may work!

In the North, you are unlikely ever to be left in circumstances where you do not have an English-speaking guide, and your guide will interpret most conversations. The quality of such interpretation varies, however, and at busy times when there are many foreign groups in town, you may find yourself with a guide whose command of English is not very good. Be patient if your meaning is not understood the first time, and remember that your guide will have had few opportunities to hear native English speakers.

Nonconfrontation

Do not be surprised if there is a lack of eye contact during conversations, or indeed at other times. Koreans do not like to look directly at people except for the shortest periods, since this is regarded as confrontational. They are not being shifty, merely polite by Korean standards. Neither do they like to begin business right away. It is polite to exchange views about the weather or the season, and you may well be asked for your impressions of the country. Questions about your health are also possible— there is no need to be too precise in replying.

Koreans will also avoid confrontation in conversations or negotiations. The use of direct negatives is avoided; better to say "There is a small problem" than to say "No." If there is a difficulty, like most people, Koreans will become somewhat uneasy and may start shifting around—it is a good idea to suggest a break at such a point.

In South Korea, politics has become less of a taboo subject than it used to be, but remember that the prevailing political ethos is very conservative by Western standards. Remember also that South Koreans are proud of the progress that they have made toward a more democratic society in recent years.

In the North, it is probably best to avoid political discussions. You will not get far, and if you are seen as in any way critical, you will cause offense. In particular, you should avoid any hostile comment about either Kim Il Sung, the founding president, or his son and the country's current leader, Kim Jong Il. Any adverse comment will certainly be taken amiss, as will any mistreatment of pictures of either leader. Do not deface or even crumple newspapers with their images. This has led to trouble for some visitors.

You will find that some subjects that might be avoided in the West will readily be brought into the conversation in Korea. Your health may well become the subject of inquiry or debate, in both

North and South. In the South, be prepared for searching questions about your religion, especially from Korean Christians. You should also note that Korean Protestants do not generally smoke or drink, and that seeing foreign Protestants doing this may cause some disquiet.

Sports is a good conversational gambit, and inquiries about families are usually well received. Pictures of family members can be a help. Where and what you have studied will usually evoke a positive response. Remember, however, that most Koreans have only heard of a few educational establishments outside their own country. Harvard, Yale, Oxford, and Cambridge may be recognized, but not much beyond. Such topics, of course, belong at social rather than business gatherings.

COMMUNICATIONS IN THE SOUTH
The Press
Since the late 1980s, the South Korean press has been free of the political controls that operated during the years of military or quasi-military rule. Radio and television are perhaps not quite so free, but they are now much more willing to air controversial subjects, especially political ones, than was the case in the past. Foreigners without Korean are well catered to with two long-established English-language papers,

the *Korean Herald* and the *Korean Times*. The former has long been seen as linked to the government, while the latter, part of the *Hankook Ilbo* (*Korean Daily*) group, has been regarded as more independent. The reality is that it is hard to see much difference between them, either in coverage or in opinions. The *Joongang Ilbo* newspaper group has a link to the *International Herald Tribune*, and publishes a version of this. These papers provide both domestic and international stories, as well as information about theaters, lectures, and so on. They also have Internet sites.

The Internet

The Internet has caught on in South Korea in a big way, and visitors will find that hotels are fully equipped for them to have access to it. Broadband is widespread. Here, however, the government is inclined to be more interventionist than it is in the West, at least in regard to some subjects. Accessing Internet sites relating to North Korea is in theory an offense under South Korea's national security laws, and some controversial political sites have been blocked. Recently the government has taken moves to deny access to some sites that carried pictures of the killing of a Korean hostage in Iraq. For foreigners, many English-language sites give information about developments in Korea and what is going on in the way of entertainment. There are also many foreign chat rooms and blogs available.

The Media
Television channels include the English-language "Arirang," which also has a Web page and an FM radio channel, and the American Forces Network, Korea (AFKN); the latter also runs a radio service. The state Korean Broadcasting System (KBS) has radio stations that specialize in classical music. In the hotels, channels such as CNN and BBC World Television, and other European or American channels, will usually be available, as will Chinese and Japanese channels.

Mail
The modern Korean postal system dates from the 1880s; a famous political event is the so-called "Post Office coup of 1884," when progressive politicians were attacked while attending a dinner marking the opening of the country's first Post Office. It is an efficient system, with cards and letters reaching the United States and Europe within a couple of days of mailing. The Post Office is also conscientious about returning undelivered mail.

Telephones

The South Korean telephone and fax system is efficient and widespread throughout the country. All hotels are on IDD.

South Korea has taken to cell phones in a big way, and two of the world's main manufacturers, LG and Samsung, are South Korean. There are claims that the 2002 presidential election was won by a determined effort via phone messages to get younger voters out to support the radical candidate, Roh Moo Hyun. Visitors will find that acquiring and operating a cell phone is easy and useful.

COMMUNICATIONS IN THE NORTH

The picture is different in North Korea. The press, radio, and television are tightly controlled, and are only available in Korean. The weekly *Pyongyang Times* newspaper and the foreign-language versions of it contain no information about what is happening in North Korea. Instead, readers receive a stream of propaganda articles that quickly begin to pall. For what may be available at theaters or the circus, visitors need to ask their guides. However, foreigners staying in some hotels in Pyongyang today can view BBC World Service Television and some Chinese channels, including Chinese Central Television's English-language channel.

The postal system appears efficient, although delays sometimes occur because of the relatively low number of international flights available from the North. The telephone and fax system provides international direct dialing and generally works well, although poor electricity supplies can interrupt the transmission of messages.

There is no access to the Internet in North Korea, although there are periodic rumors that this will arrive "soon." North Korean sponsored sites based in China, Japan, and Germany have emerged, however. For a brief period in 2002, foreigners were allowed to bring in cell phones, even though they could not be used. This seemed to be in anticipation of the introduction of a domestic mobile system. There were reports that this was introduced in 2003 for Korean officials, but that it was closed down in June 2004. The current position for foreign visitors is that such phones are still being taken away at points of entry.

CONCLUSION

Here is a peninsula of spectacular natural beauty, with mountains, landscapes, and seascapes that can match anything elsewhere in the world. Seoul or Pyongyang may not have many historical remains, but both reward their visitors in different ways. A cultural center in its own right, Korea has also played a major role in forging links between mainland and island East Asia. It was the channel for, and the interpreter of, Chinese culture for Japan. Its pottery has been the envy of both Chinese and Japanese potters since the tenth century.

Modern Korea has seen two very different political and economic experiments. South Korea's development has been astounding, as a visit to its vibrant cities and modern industrial complexes will quickly demonstrate. North Korea is in some ways equally remarkable, as one of the few surviving relics of the Marxist-Leninist experiment that began in Russia in 1917, but which here has developed in very different ways.

In addition, the Koreans themselves are worth getting to know better. These are tough people, who have resisted all attempts by powerful neighbors to dominate them or to take over their territory. They can come across as determined and firm, but they respond well to the hand of friendship. Whether North or South, Koreans take to those who persist in getting to know them. Go frequently, and before long you are an old friend, entitled to special consideration. They will be demanding, sometimes overwhelmingly so, but if they believe that you are on their side, they will do everything possible to help you.

Further Reading

Breen, Michael. *The Koreans: Who They Are, What They Want, Where Their Future Lies.* London: Orion Business Books, 1998.

Crowder Han, Suzanne. *Notes on Things Korean.* Seoul, and Elizabeth, NJ: Hollym, 1996.

Cumings, Bruce. *Korea's Place in the Sun: A Modern History.* New York and London: W.W. Norton, 1997.

————. *North Korea: Another Country.* New York and London: The New Press, 2004.

De Mente, Boyé. *NTC's Dictionary of Korea's Business and Cultural Code Words.* Chicago: NTC, 1998.

Foreign Languages Publishing House, eds. *Korea in the 20th Century.* Pyongyang: FLPH, 2002.

Hoare, James, and Susan Pares. *Conflict in Korea: An Encyclopedia.* Santa Barbara, CA, Denver, CO, and Oxford: ABC-CLIO, 1999.

Hur, Sonja Vegdhal, and Ben Seunghwa Hur. *Culture Shock! Korea: A Guide to Customs and Etiquette.* Portland, Oregon: Graphic Arts Center Publishing, 2003/London: Kuperard, 2003.

Kim, Ilpyong J. *Historical Dictionary of North Korea.* Lanham, MD, and Oxford: Scarecrow Press Inc., 2003.

Kohls, L. Robert. *Learning to Think Korean: A Guide to Living and Working in Korea.* Yarmouth, ME: Intercultural Press, 2001.

Korea National Tourism Organization, eds. *Korea Travel Guide.* Seoul: KNTO, 2003.

Korean Overseas Information Service, eds. *Facts about Korea.* Seoul: KOIS, 2003.

Lee, Ki-baik. *A New History of Korea.* Translated by Edward Willet Wagner, with Edward J. Schultz. Cambridge, MA, and London: Harvard University Press, 1984.

Nahm, Andrew J., and James Hoare. *Historical Dictionary of the Republic of Korea.* Lanham, MD, and Oxford: Scarecrow Press Inc., 2nd edition, 2004.

Oberdorfer, Don. *The Two Koreas: A Contemporary History.* London: Little, Brown and Co., 1998.

Portal, Jane. *Art and Archaeology of Korea.* London: British Museum Press, 2000.

Pratt, Keith, and Richard Rutt. *Korea: A Historical and Cultural Dictionary.* Richmond, Surrey: Curzon Press, 1999.

Springer, Chris. *Pyongyang: The Hidden History of the North Korean Capital.* Budapest: Entente Bt., 2003.

Willoughby, Robert. *North Korea: The Bradt Travel Guide.* Chalfont St. Peter, Bucks, UK: Bradt Travel Guides, 2003.

Yonhap News Agency, eds. *Korea Annual: A Comprehensive Handbook on Korea: Appendix North Korea.* Seoul: Yonhap News Agency, 40th Annual edition, 2003.

In-Flight Korean. New York: Living Language, 2001.

Complete Korean. New York: Living Language, 2007.

culture smart! korea

Index